Hanging Plants

by John Philip Baumgardt

Other books by John Philip Baumgardt HOW TO PRUNE ALMOST EVERYTHING
BULBS FOR SUMMER BLOOM

for Home,
Terrace,
and Garden

A FIRESIDE BOOK published by SIMON AND SCHUSTER

First paperback edition 1974

SBN 671-21189-7 Casebound
SBN 671-21762-3 Paperback
Library of Congress Catalog Card Number: 72-76406
Designed by Edith Fowler
Manufactured in the United States of America

2   3   4   5   6   7   8   9   10

Contents

My Trailing Favorites

It's too bad I wasn't born a grand duke, or at least the junior assistant undergardener of a grand duke, because I love plants that trail, droop, and dangle—and these look best in great urns set in formal gardens or as weeping standards (have you ever *seen* a standard of a pendent fuchsia?) or in great, luxuriant baskets in a handsome conservatory.

Still, I enjoy my own decumbent plants. In the house, trailers such as the episcias, grape-ivy relatives, and scindapsus grow in the windows. At my north entrance, baskets of fuchsias have been known to spread to nearly 4 feet in a single summer. More baskets of petunias, begonias, and assorted experimental plantings hang in dappled shade above the terrace. In my little greenhouse some orchids swing overhead, happily growing in baskets side by side with the huge staghorn fern, baskets of oxalis, gesneriads, and several other tender treasures. This is a fair accomplishment for the Middle West because, while wind is anathema to all plants, it is especially deadly for fully exposed hanging plants, and my garden is wind-swept. In summer the temperature may stay over 100° F. for days on end. My baskets may not be as succulent looking and floriferous as those in Seattle; still, they please me and make the visitors to my garden both appreciative and envious.

Downward-growing plants have a special sort of charm, rather like the graceful sag of the Venus De Milo's garments. I shall never, never forget my first hypocyrta. Here was this handsome little plant with sprawling stems loaded with pairs of shiny leaves for all the world like halves of small olives. I was away for a few days, and when I returned the plant was swimming with goldfish! It's true! Inch-and-a-half long brilliant orange tubular flowers had sprung up here and there from the leaf joints, and they were shaped exactly like pudgy goldfish, complete with gold lips. I was ever more floored the time a stanhopia orchid bloomed through the *hole in the bottom of the pot* (it went into a basket quickly) . But these are special cases. The real fun with pendent plants is living with them day by day. They belong in the house, in the plant room or greenhouse, and in the garden.

Let me urge you to do a good job of planting pendent plants; they deserve a high-quality, unobtrusive container (unless you run to marble urns) and carefully compounded potting composts. After you have the plants going, visit them frequently to tend to their needs. Water quite often and supply sufficient fertilizer to keep growth coming on but without stimulating leaves at the expense of flowers. If you become interested in fuchsias, lantanas, and other choice woody plants, it won't be long before you will be investing in a small backyard greenhouse to carry them over from year to year.

A friend of mine has all of her fuchsias named—not varietal names, but family names: Clarice, Winifred, and Bubbles are a few I seem to recall. But then I once had a dear neighbor who named all of her great clumps of Bath delphiniums after deceased relatives, too. We run to that sort of thing in these parts.

Don't rush out and buy a planted basket. Do start with a few small, easy house plants for the window ledge and in mid-spring plant up a basket of petunias or nasturtiums for your first attempt at pendent plants. Then graduate to the more exotic and demanding sorts. Before long, your garden will take on a new look; plants fore and aft, right and left, and overhead. That's what we want—plants overhead. What could be nicer than to be completely surrounded by flowers?

JOHN PHILIP BAUMGARDT

Kansas City, Missouri
February, 1972

1

The Exciting Third Dimension

A long, sunlit vista of flowers is a wonderful sight, especially if a broad sweep of blossoming plants lies at our feet. Add an overhead cascade of pendent plants and the miracle is complete. We are in a world of flowers. We are surrounded by the beauty of floral forms, floral colors, and floral scent. While gardeners commonly plant in broad beds and design views with great depth, overhead possibilities often are overlooked.

Have you ever walked through a great public conservatory where wire baskets of wonderful viny things and beautiful flowering plants hung overhead? Or walked the steep hillsides of San Francisco, looking up at the tiny balconies with overhead wires garlanded with ivy geraniums, or cypress vine, or morning-glories? Have you visited Munich at Oktoberfest time and sat under a bower of silver-lace-vine growing out of old beer kegs set right on the sidewalk? There is a nostalgia connected with overhead flowers, a special grace to pendent plants. This exciting vertical dimension of horticulture is easy to achieve. You can do it with annuals or with perennials; you can do it in the garden or in the living room. It is a dimension for the country estate, for the modest city backyard or for the apartment dweller's window. By all means, if you love plants and like to garden, think of plants overhead—plants spilling down from baskets or cascading from boxes.

Left, a rattan bird cage, attractively planted with *Episcia* 'Green Gold' and the house ivy, *Hedera helix* 'Curlilocks'. Actually, the plants are in a shallow bulb pan set in the lower half of the wickerwork.

Middle, tomatoes in a basket; a delightful idea for a hanging-basket planting near the kitchen door. Choose a large basket and fill with a porous soil mixture. The tomato plant should be a dwarf variety or one of the "cherry" sort, as shown. Pinch the plant frequently as it develops to make a branching specimen.

Right, *Hoya bella* growing in a hanging container made of redwood sticks laid up log-cabin fashion. Handsome as a house plant the year round, *Hoya bella* produces heads of charming red-and-white flowers intermittently. Note the basket link made in the form of a monkey that joins the basket chains to the brass bracket.

"UP" COMPLEMENTS WIDTH AND DEPTH

Capability Brown, Le Nôtre, and Gertrude Jekyll, among other great garden designers, all knew the value of overhead plants and of cascading flowers. Their gardens often were laid out to be viewed from an arbor or pergola where vines grow overhead and from which baskets of flowers may be suspended. These gardens often feature a strategically placed urn with gay blooms tumbling down the sides and with a strong vertical line ascending from the central point. They knew the value of well-placed standards of fuchsia, geranium, lantana, rose, heliotrope, cape plumbago, and other species, and all the better if the standard was a weeping form. We see traces of this feeling for overhead color in the high swags of roses at Bagatelle and in Regent's Park, in the colorful terrace gardens of Mainau Island in Lake Constance, in the urns that glorify public places in Paris, London, and Berlin, as well as in the window boxes of European villages.

Tropical plants in the garden. The left figure shows orchids and other epiphytes growing happily on the limb of a tree in a Miami garden. The plants were wired onto mats of fiber, then secured to the trees. The middle photo shows *Rhoeo discolor* growing on the trunk of a palm tree, where it developed from a windblown seed. A bromeliad, right, wired with a wad of sphagnum moss to a piece of driftwood hangs against a rough-textured building. All of these may be used as ornamentals in northern gardens so long as they are taken indoors during cold weather.

But overhead flowers are not an exclusive achievement of European gardeners. The roof gardens of New York and San Francisco drip flowers. Wonderful new pendent fuchsias and tuberous begonias originate every year in northern California, Oregon, and Washington, and the gardeners of that horticulturally blessed coast use them freely in their gardens. Great American botanic gardens, such as Longwood and Calloway, make a point of exhibiting perfect specimens of tender and hardy hanging plants, plants in baskets and plants in boxes and urns. The Brooklyn Botanic Garden and Missouri Botanic Garden give a course each year, teaching homeowners how to properly prepare and plant hanging baskets. Porch box and window box how-to-do-it articles fill the garden magazines along about March. Mr. Newly Wed brings his bride a magnificently

grown pendent fuchsia in a basket on their first anniversary, and she wonders how on earth to care for it.

To go from the general to the specific, you can find a place for overhead and pendent plants in your garden. You may place a pair of Dutch benches on each side of the kitchen door and build a trellis up over them to carry vines and a basket or two. You may decide to include window-box brackets under the windows when you talk house design with your architect. If you are an indoor gardener with window shelves full of African-violets (like mine), you may add a few episcias, columneas, and hypocyrtas for a magic cascade of graceful foliage and glowing flowers. If your home is contemporary

Two dry-climate plants for indoor culture are, far left, Rhipsalis, a cactus relative, and, left, a bromeliad, a relative of the pineapple. Both plants are characterized by strong lines; both are planted in contemporary earthenware containers with low-gloss glazes in earthy tones to compliment the plants. Both specimens grow in the Chestnut Hill home of Ernesta Drinker Ballard.

and not at all given to frills, try a modern ceramic container with a formal, weeping, tropical foliage plant—a scindapsus, or a *Sedum morganianum*—or feature a huge basket of *Hoya carnosa varietaga* in an important window.

The best instruction is a good example according to the pedagogues, and the best example of good use of pendent plants that I have seen in a house and a home garden is at Ernesta and Fred Ballard's in Chestnut Hill, Pennsylvania. The marble-floored entry hall features a marvelous array of house plants, from huge to quite small, all perfectly grown and groomed. An unusual pottery container with a rare trailing rhipsalis hangs in the window. In the

The constantly renewed, single orange blossoms of *Begonia sutherlandii* sparkle against the neat, angel-wing-type foliage of this handsome decumbent plant. Grown in dappled sunlight in the garden through the summer months, this species goes right on blooming when it moves into a bright window for the winter. Ample moisture and frequent feeding insure success.

living-room window, where a fine grouping of tropical plants occupies a window sill, a bracket-hung tillandsia supplies the "up" dimension. Where the choicest house plants line up before the French doors in the dining room, a trellised hoya and a climbing fern, allowed to climb a pole and then cascade, supply the pendent quality.

In the Ballard garden a long grape arbor supports baskets of begonias, fuchsias, Swedish-ivy, and other outdoor (in summer) beauties. On the terrace, high standards of weeping fuchsias sway with Edwardian grace, and wonderful urns of *Lantana sellowiana* and sprawling *Plumbago capensis* catch the eye. It is such a *natural* placement of uniquely formed plant materials. Every hanging plant looks just right for where it is. The point is, the vertical lines of these pendent and overhead plants compliment the width and breadth of other elements of the garden design. They give the final touch.

BASKETS, SHELF BRACES, AND PEDESTALS

When you decide to add a hanging basket or a window box to your collection, forgo things that are cute. Keep in mind your beautiful plant. You don't want anything to detract from it. Your basket should be a simple wire one, very strong and preferably painted dark green. The best ones come from England and are advertised in garden magazines. Fine chain makes better hangers than wire, and English baskets come with chain in most cases. Or you can go to the hardware shop and buy brass furnace chain, spray-paint it green, and it will survive to support your grandchildren's baskets. The hardware store is also the place to get sturdy brackets and shelf braces. My preference is for a swinging brass-wire bracket with about a 15-inch arm for outdoor baskets that hang next to a wall. And I like heavy aluminum shelf brackets for the windows, as they can be painted to match the sills. A local glass shop provides 6- or 8-inch-wide glass shelving with a beaded front edge cut to needed lengths. Three glass shelves and a swinging arm bracket or two for hanging plants turn any window into a true winter garden.

Pedestals are coming back into style and furniture manufacturers are again offering them. Recently American of Chicago sent me a brochure about a walnut-burl single-pedestal plant stand—the 15-inch-square box was tin lined—and I promptly bought one. What a treasure! Every time a window plant or something in the little greenhouse out back reaches its prime, into the box it goes with a bit of background in the way of potted maidenhair fern, sansevieria or myrtle, and a pocket-sized "hanging garden" greets the vistior in the entryway. Nothing seems more attractive than a slender column with a lovely cascading plant. You may have just the place for such a *pièce de resistance* in your home.

Two trailing plants in one plant-lover's home. *Columnea arguta,* left, grows in a perforated ceramic container; during winter months its bright red blossoms brighten the room. The gesneriad, *Episcia* 'Noel', right, displays its chocolate metallic foliage well in a small wall basket.

2

Handsome Hanging House Plants

Enthusiastic growers of house plants have them everywhere; on shelves in the windows, on brackets screwed to the sills, on the mantel, in the entryway—anywhere a plant can grow. Most plants like kitchen and bathroom windows. Scattered among upright-growing specimens are ivies, hoyas, episcias, ferns, and other delightful plants that droop, trail, or dangle. These are the ones that add the finishing touch to a collection—that give style and grace. But you don't have to be a full-time indoor gardener to take advantage of this. One well-grown sweet-potato vine cascading down a window sill adds charm to a room. A single, well-grown specimen of iron-hardy airplane-plant on the newel, on a pedestal, or on the edge of a table makes a house homelike. Get one trailing plant and learn to live with it. Soon you will want more.

The trick to growing trailing plants (or any other kind, for that matter) indoors is to match the plant to the environment. If a thermometer set on the window ledge of your living-room window tells you that the temperature there runs near 72° in the day and 5 to 10 degrees cooler at night, and if you know that the room is nearly as dry as the Sahara desert, and the window in question gets at least dappled sunlight on bright winter days, you can intelligently select an appropriate plant. Let's consider where trailing plants can be grown to advantage in the average home.

All plants need light, and plenty of it. Unless you plan to use plant-growth light fixtures that provide auxiliary light artificially, plan to keep all your plants within 3 feet of a window. Those that want bright sun should go right in the window. Dime-store brackets and plate-glass shelves from a glazier's shop can turn any window into an up-and-down garden. Old-fashioned or contemporary swinging brackets may be fastened one above the other on window frames. I favor the substantial cast-iron ones, as they support a largish pot saucer to catch the drip and save the floor. Bracket arms, meant to support a hanging basket, jardiniere, or even a birdcage may be mounted over a window so container and plant are directly opposite the light.

Inside a room, you can use a tier table, an old-fashioned bent-wire multilevel plant stand or a book shelf at right angles to the glass. All these hold lots of plants; probably you will have to rotate them frequently, as those farthest into the room will reach for the light.

If you are an average homeowner who just wants a plant or two around, why not settle for an easy window-sill garden? The surest and easiest way is to procure a metal or plastic tray the dimensions of the sill, fill it with ornamental river stones and bring water up almost to the top of the stones. Invert two or three clean terra-cotta flower pots on the pebbles; these will become pedestals for your pendent plants.

What about that tray of water? This is an important feature of house-plant gardening. Plants like, want, demand, high humidity. The average home has low humidity. A tray of water under plants provides a constant wash of water vapor for the foliage, and plants do better.

But, you say, you want a grape-ivy to cascade down the beautiful antique library steps in the corner? And there is no window? There is no way to grow an ivy on those steps, but that does not mean you cannot have one there from time to time. Get a nice plant from the florist and grow it into a lovely specimen in the kitchen window. When visitors are expected, whisk it into the living room and onto the steps. Drape it artfully in place—and you have grape-ivy on your antique library steps. The point is, you cannot *grow* plants deep into a room or in dark corners. You can grow them at the windows, and move them around according to the demands of your decoration.

The spring flower show helps amateur gardeners develop their ideas. This collection of minature plants, grown by the director of the Pennsylvania Horticultural Society, includes species that do well together and that are manageable by a beginning gardener. The hanging potted plant at the left is *Episcia dianthifolia*. The small basket on the right is completely masked by the luxuriant foliage of baby's-tears.

I must interrupt to tell you a story. A friend of mine is an African-violet fiend. Her basement, fitted with fluorescent lights, is jammed with hundreds of dishpan-sized, blue-ribbon specimens. When she learned that there were other gesneriads (African-violets are in the *Gesneriaceae*) such as the episcias, columneas, hypocyrtas, and the like, she fell in love with these pendent kinds and soon added a vast array of them to her collection. At this point, the basement was beautiful beyond belief—but visitors are never allowed below stairs. Every evening, large basket in hand, she visits her subterranean garden and selects three African-violets and five pendent plants. These go upstairs to spend the evening with the family (and sometimes friends). One African-violet goes on the drum table with the large reading lamp, another in a jardiniere on the hall console, and the third one on the coffee table. The pendent plants are placed in well-lit spots: two or three on the book shelves, one on a window shelf, and another on the mantel. Before retiring, she carries them to the basement again. She says it is less trouble than airing the two terriers.

Window garden in a downtown office. A small basket of artillery plant, and larger baskets of (top) grape-ivy and *Davallia* ferns soften the window of Ernesta D. Ballard's office in the fine old Philadelphia house occupied by the Pennsylvania Horticultural Society. The large tubbed plant is a mature specimen of the lady palm.

Where are *my* indoor danglers? My very bright breakfast room is mostly windows; two have four glass shelves each, and these are filled with plants. The wide sill of another is reserved for the colored-leaf episcias, hypocyrtas, and the like. One dining-room window has glass shelves, and these always carry several plants. The kitchen window is host to a few more, and at least one group planting and a single plant live on the serving shelf under fluorescent light. One bathroom window upstairs has its plants, several more live under artificial light in the basement, and various ivies, airplane-plants, and others that like it bright and cool inhabit the laundry-room windows. In my little backyard greenhouse there is one of everything and several of some. It is never a problem to find a suitable plant to decorate a table when visitors are expected.

These are easy foliage plants: the true ivies, the *Hedera* species, house-plant forms with small, closely placed leaves; the grape-ivies, *Cissus* species, including the almost indestructible kangaroo-vine, antarctic-ivy, and common grape-ivy; ivy-arum, the common name

A gardener's indoor garden requires special preparation. Watertight metal (use plastic, if you wish) trays filled with pebbles and water rest on the wide window ledge. Plants thrive on the humidity created by this arrangement. Overhead baskets contain a grape-ivy, a pellionia, and a begonia. In the trays, decumbent plants are raised on inverted pots.

for *Scindapsus areus* and its variety 'Marble Queen', known to most folks as pothos or "the philodendron with the speckled leaves"; the *Asparagus* species, including the asparagus-fern and *A. sprengeri*, a weeping coleus or two—these go in bright, cool windows; Swedish-ivy, *Plectranthus oertendahlii* and its variegated form, and the good old striped airplane-plant, *Chlorophytum*.

For growing right on the window sill, we can add to this list the zebrinas (wandering Jew), the rosary-vine relatives, *Ceropegia* species, perhaps one or two others, but these, while intriguing, scarcely are beautiful enough to come under a recommended list of best plants. All of the above are easy to obtain (the grocery store probably will have them sooner or later) and easy to care for. Given water almost daily, bright light, and a little house-plant fertilizer while they are making new growth, they should last for years.

Some showy tropical pendent plants delight in the heat and humidity of kitchen or bathroom. These want plenty of light, but also *very high humidity* and constant warmth. Among the gesneriads are nut-orchids (*Achimenes* species and hybrids), hypocyrtas, and episcias. The pellionias, pileas (some with flowers as well as beautiful foliage), and most basket-type tropical ferns are in this category. All require a very porous compost, frequent watering, and frequent feeding with a dilute fertilizer solution.

If you are blessed with a plant room, a cool sun porch, or a spare bedroom, kept cool and with a bright window, you can enjoy Kenilworth-ivy, *Cymbalaria muralis;* the ivy-geraniums (these are among the most beautiful of house plants, but they demand bright light and a temperature between 55° and 65°F., nothing higher); piggyback plant, *Tolmiea menziesii,* and the basket oxalises.

Whether your house-plant collection numbers one or one hundred, take care of each plant and keep it growing. Visit your plants every day with watering can in hand. Give each a splash, a drop, or a drench, according to its needs. Turn each one slightly to keep it symmetrical, and clip off tired foliage and spent blossoms, if any. Two or three times a month, move your plants to kitchen sink or shower and wash their leaves.

Before leaving this topic of trailing plants in the house, let's dispose of a question or two. Somebody is sure to ask about philodendrons. The fact is, most philodendrons are conservatory plants, not adaptable to house conditions. And the few that tolerate, or do well in, house and office are not the pendent sorts. Vining philodendrons deteriorate in the average home. The new leaves get smaller and smaller, and the plants look dreadful. Stay with *Scindapsus* 'Marble Queen'.

What about baskets of fuchsias, lantanas, geraniums, and similar flowering plants that filled Grandma's windows? Build a bay window like Grandma's, and cool your house to 60°F. like Grandma's (remember how everyone huddled around the stove?), and you can have them—also you can have baskets of nasturtiums, browallia, begonias, lobelia, and lots of other things. Today we reserve these for the garden room or greenhouse because we prefer our living rooms too warm for them. They are all very easy—all it takes is a cool, bright room. If you have a warm, bright room and can raise the humidity to at least 30 percent, try a basket wreathed with passion-flower vines. There are many kinds, one prettier than the other.

3

Dictionary of Indoor Trailers

Your home offers several places suitable for plant growing. One plant or another will thrive in any window; if you put shelves across the window panes, you will enjoy a living screen of foliage, all the more attractive if at least some of the plants trail. Grow plants on a stand at the entryway; on brackets at eye level where you work in the kitchen; in a basket on the landing of the stairs. The following list will help you choose plants to fit the environmental conditions you have to offer.

Make a conscious effort to develop a sensitivity to your plants' needs. If the plant persists in bending toward the window, obviously it is telling you that it wants more light; if it is dry every time you look, it needs more frequent watering or a soil mixture more retentive of moisture. Pale foliage may indicate a need for fertilizer; bleached foliage is pale from too much light. With experience you will find these things out for yourself.

Often in this list of plants I say that a plant takes "average room conditions." And I mean just that: the plant is able to grow where people—today's people—are comfortable, as far as humidity and temperature are concerned. Occasionally the term "charcoal" is mentioned. Charcoal from hardwood is extremely absorbent; in a soil mix it takes up toxic chemicals and holds them so they cannot harm nearby roots. If you have to use highly mineralized water for your plants, bits of hardwood charcoal (see Glossary) mixed through the potting compost make all the difference between success and failure. But do not crumble charcoal briquets meant for the backyard broiler. These contain binding ingredients that are damaging to plants.

Do you know what a dibble is? Surely every gardener must; bulb catalogues always list dibbles. These are pointed tools, rather like a piece of broomstick that has been pointed pencil-fashion, and are meant for making holes to plant in. The verb, too, is dibble. You dibble in the pansies, using your dibble. If you want to place a plant in the side of your basket (through the moss) , you make a hole with a dibble, insert the plant, then, with your fingers, work the soil and moss back into place. Other terms that may perplex are found in the Glossary.

Achimenes Nut-orchid   Gesneriad Family
These make nice baskets and pendent pot plants for the house. They are quite easy under lights. (See also Chapter 5.)

Abutilon Flowering-maple   Mallow Family
A. megapotamicum and its variety with variegated leaves make fine hanging plants for the summer garden. The potting compost is 2 parts loam, 1 part each peat and sand. Grow in full to nearly full sun, preferably out of wind; water freely so soil never dries. While this woody plant tends to climb, it may be trained downward. The yellow-and-scarlet blossoms appear throughout summer. To carry over your plant, move it to a sunny window in a cool room; prune slightly when you bring it indoors, and heavily in March. Early spring cuttings root readily in sandy soil under a plastic cover at 70° F. Abutilon responds to any sort of fertilizer, but feeding is not necessary if the potting compost includes good loam. (Details in Chapter 6.)

Asparagus Asparagus-fern; Sprengeri   Lily Family
Who has not grown *A. sprengeri* and *A. plumosus* (the asparagus-fern) in porch boxes, urns, and hanging baskets? They go

straight back to the heyday of Victorian conservatories and have been with us ever since. All indoor and ornamental-garden sorts are easy. The best potting compost is 2 parts loam and 1 part of a mixture of equal parts leafmold, brown peat, and fine sand. Force into active growth by repotting and watering in March; as new growth begins, apply liquid manure or fish emulsion solution every month. Keep the soil damp through summer but allow to dry slightly between waterings from October to March. During hot weather, syringe the foliage daily. Easy to grow from seed, but most home gardeners propagate these by dividing older plants. Actually climbing plants, the tropical asparagus ornamentals tend to trail when grown in pots or baskets. They are good companion plants for something with showy flowers. They also make excellent specimens.

Try a basket with smilax, *Asparagus asparagoides*. The glossy leaves are beautiful in themselves, and this is a house plant you can cut freely while in good growth. *A. crispus* and *A. meyeri* are becoming popular again. Both are easy to grow; both make outstanding specimens for hanging in a bright window over the winter and in dappled sunlight in the garden in summer.

Begonia   Begonia Family

Most begonias except the cane-forming kinds make suitable basket plants (tuberous begonias are discussed in Chapter 7). A select list of especially handsome basket species is given here, and these, too, may go to the garden for the summer, where they grow in dappled shade with frequent watering and biweekly feeding. Buy small plants to get a start. Increase their number by rooting small side shoots in sand or water. Grow in pots until blooming sized, then replant in 10- to 12-inch baskets, one per container. The best potting compost is equal parts loam and leafmold plus half a part each dried cow manure and fine sand. All do well at average room temperature, with humidity as high as possible, and in fairly bright light. For strong flowering, some sun is essential.

Recommended species include *B. digwelliana, B. foliosa, B. fuchsioides,* and *B. sutherlandii*. The last, with its sprays of half-inch brilliant orange flowers, may be kept in full flower most of the year. It is wonderful, indoors and out.

A collection of leaves from rex begonia seedlings; the rhizomatous begonias are among the best basket plants for the house. They live a long time and the foliage is colorful and handsome the year round.

A very easy plant for the beginner is *Begonia foliosa.* This leafy species with drooping stems and tiny, starry flowers starts readily from a slip rooted in a glass of water. It will develop into a grand plant in your south or east window.

The lightly patterned *Saxifraga sarmentosa,* sometimes called strawberry-begonia, is hardy outdoors and a well-behaved house plant. Useful in baskets, it is also wonderful for the strawberry jar. From time to time sprays of small pink flowers hover over the leaves like tiny butterflies.

The basket is made of native cork, the effect charmingly rustic. This is a composition of foliage colors and textures, featuring the rex begonia 'Louise Closson', the florists' maidenhair fern, artillery plant, and a second begonia, 'Wild Grapes'.

Bromeliads, Epiphytic Types   Pineapple Family

I suppose that most of the bromeliads qualify as basket plants; at least, in nature they grow overhead, and the flowers or leaves or both may be somewhat pendent. While these do not look well mingled with broadleaf plants, they do fit into the cactus window nicely. Most are epiphytic, a few grow in a humusy substrate; place pot brackets up the sides of the window frame and hang the pots in these. Or select a nicely formed piece of driftwood to hang in the window. Here and there tie on clumps of fibrous sphagnum moss or orchid fiber that has been pulled apart. Wire various bromeliads (epiphytic varieties only) to these growing sites, including a little more moss or fiber around the base.

You can force your bromeliads to bloom almost at will. The funnel of leaves of the epiphytic bromeliads should always be filled with water, while the root system is just kept from bone dryness. Set an apple (not variety 'Delicious') in the funnel, and cover the entire plant with a plastic bag. Leave in place for several days. The apple produces a gas that is absorbed by the water, then by the plant, stimulating the production of a flower shoot. A few crumbs of calcium carbide (from the drugstore) dropped into the water in the plant's funnel usually does the same thing. In the case of the apple, the gas is ethylene; carbide produces acetylene.

All bromeliads appreciate 75° to 80° F. warmth, with a very high humidity. Some, particularly the epiphytic types, tolerate average room conditions.

Cacti   Cactus Family

Several of the cacti are more or less pendent and are good plants for basket or hanging-pot culture.

Epiphyllum. Most plants grown under this name belong in other genera listed below. *E. ackermannii,* rose-red, probably still belongs in this genus. And some of the hybrids sold as orchid-cacti have *Epiphyllum* somewhere in their breeding. Pot in equal parts loam, peat, and leafmold, and add a trace of sand. Grow in the garden over the summer, in a *cold* spare bedroom (no light at night) in the winter. Water sparingly always. Feed with any house-plant fertilizer solution through the summer months.

Rhipsalis. These apparently leafless, often decumbent plants seem to be put together of fleshy green sticks like a child's tinker toy. They have little beauty and are a challenge to grow. The potting compost is equal parts loam, leafmold, crushed brick, and sand. Line the basket with osmunda (orchid fiber) cut in very thin sheets so drainage will be perfect. Temperature and watering as for *Epiphyllum,* but grow somewhat drier over winter.

Schlumbergera. The Easter cactus, Christmas cactus and relatives belong in this group. Compost is the same as for *Epiphyllum,* and the care is the same. New hybrids of this genus are strong growers with magnificent flowers. But if you bring them into the living room to enjoy their beauty, buds and blossoms will promptly drop. You must visit them in the cold room where no light is used at night.

Zygocactus. The Thanksgiving cactus and its many cultivars and hybrids belong in this group. Grow these as *Epiphyllum* and *Schlumbergera.* For best flowers, grow as cool as possible in early fall; a north window is best. When buds first appear, add very dilute fertilizer solution to the water.

All these cacti propagate from cuttings stuck in potting mix.

Calathea (including *Maranta*)   Prayer-plant   Arrowroot Family

These are rather broad-leaved plants, foliage usually handsomely mottled, often slightly clasping. Upright stems grow from basal crown, occasionally rather creeping. Plant in a compost of equal parts loam, peat, leafmold, and sand, with old cow manure freely added. Difficult for the home, they are beautiful in the warm, humid conditions of the plant room or greenhouse. Water to keep evenly moist, fertilize when plants are in active growth.

These are handsome when dibbled into the sides of a hanging basket; they seem to enjoy the moisture that evaporates from the moss, and the leaves take on extra color. Select sorts include *Calathea insignis, C. ornata* and its varieties, *C. makoyana* and *C. zebrina binotii, Maranta leuconeura massangeana,* and *M. leuconeura kerchoveana.*

From the florist, buy a basket plant of *Campanula isophylla*. Move it to a cool, shady place in the garden (still in its container) over summer and bring it back in the fall for another flowering in late winter.

Campanula Bluebell   Bluebell Family

Bluebells grown indoors thrive in equal parts loam, sand, and peat or leafmold. Indoor kinds include *C. fragilis, C. isophylla,* and *C. isophylla alba.* The first two are lilac-blue, the variety is white; all are gently trailing. Repot these in March, in 4- to 6-inch pots or in small baskets; water moderately in winter, generously the rest of the year. Well grown, these tender campanulas are completely covered with half-dollar-sized shallow cuplike blossoms for weeks in early spring. They want a cool room—not exceeding 60° F.—and a very bright window. Direct sunlight should be limited. As a pendent shelf or hanging-basket plant, these are hard to beat, but they really do best when brought into flower in a cool greenhouse or plant room.

Ceropegia Rosary-vine, String-of-hearts   Milkweed Family

Nothing less like a milkweed could be imagined. Most of the trailing members of this genus consist of purplish, limp, stringlike

The airplane-plant is old hat, but still valuable for indoor and outdoor decoration. Use it in pots on brackets, in baskets, and in boxes and urns. Let the children have the offsets to root in pots of damp sand.

stems with small, paired leaves spaced at wide intervals. Occasionally a plant will produce small potatolike tubers at the joints, and when these are planted, you have more vines. Rarely does the vine produce a most peculiar, nondescript brown-and-dull-purple flower that gives rise, amazingly, to an outsized milkweed seed pod. The *toute ensemble* is scarcely worth the trouble—not that they are any trouble.

Pot these in a compost of 1 part each loam, leafmold, peat, and sand. When the plant is in active growth, water with liquid manure or fish-emulsion solution. Let the soil become dry on top between waterings, and grow in partial shade in the window of a warm room. Cultivated kinds include *C. barkleyi, C. caffrorum, C. debilis,* and *C. woodii.* There are many more, but these are mostly upright growers.

Chlorophytum   Spider-plant; Airplane-plant   Lily Family

Good old airplane-plant—everybody's grandma had one in the bay window, and it spent the summer on the shady veranda. The common one is *C. comosum* var. *vittatum*. This is the sort with creamy-white striping on the daylily-like leaves that produces small plantlets on the ends of the flower scapes (hence, airplane-plant). There are other species of chlorophytum and several more varieties of *C. comosum* all worth growing as basket plants, but only the airplane-plant produces offsets on the flower stalks.

Grow in a compost of equal parts loam, peat, leafmold, and sand. Average room conditions are adequate; these plants thrive in a plant room or greenhouse. Any window location supplies sufficient light; direct sun is not essential but gives a stronger specimen. Water sparingly over winter, freely in the warm months. Divide in spring; when new growth begins, push with liquid fertilizer biweekly. This is a nice plant for the edge of a garden urn or for shady window boxes. Repot in a hanging basket to decorate the house over winter. Offsets offer an easy means of propagation; pot them up and most will root. Or root them in water or damp sand and pot up when roots are ½ inch long.

Cissus   Grape-ivy   Grape Family
These tender climbers grow best at cool room temperature, except *C. discolor,* which wants warmth. All thrive in high humidity. Moderate light—as in a north window—is adequate. The potting compost is equal parts loam, leafmold, damp, crumbly brown peat, and fine sand. Water moderately through winter months, generously through summer. Add fertilizer solution to the water while plants are making new growth. To propagate these, take cuttings of young growth with a heel of old stem; dip in mild rooting hormone powder and stick in perlite-peat mixture under a plastic cover with moderately bright light, at 75° F. All make fine pendent basket or pot plants. *C. discolor* is a strongly ascending vine and must be pruned frequently and trained, when basket grown. Among the best kinds are *C. adenopoda, C. antarctica, C. discolor* (with handsome mottled foliage) , *C. gloriosa,* and *C. rhombifolia,* the familiar grape-ivy.

Coleus   Mint Family
Given full sun indoors and a little shade in the garden, these are among the plants with brightest foliage. Start from seed or root

cuttings in peat and perlite, and grow plants in equal parts loam, peat, and sand. Keep evenly moist and fertilize biweekly. Most kinds are suitable for urns, boxes, and baskets, but the selections from hybrids of *C. rehneltianus* that are decumbent, such as 'Trailing Queen', are most suitable. As a window-sill plant that trails, these are quite good, and they also look well on the fern stand, adding color to an otherwise all-green composition. Buy choice plants from specialists; if you take your own cuttings, be sure to choose shoots with bright leaves, as there is apt to be considerable variation.

Cymbalaria   Kenilworth-ivy   Figwort Family
    Most of the cymbalarias are perfectly hardy in the garden; if you enjoy delicate, trailing plants, by all means, start *C. muralis*, Kenilworth-ivy, and *C. pallida* between the stones or bricks on the shady side of your garden wall. These and *C. aequitriloba, C. hepaticifolia,* and *C. pilosa* all make charming, delicate trailing plants for indoor growing. The stems are almost hairlike, the leaves are roundish with lobes, with or without teeth. Tiny blossoms reminiscent of snapdragons, usually lavender, bluish, or blush, appear throughout most of the year from the axils of the leaves. These plants may be grown as specimens in a small container; or use them as underplantings in baskets of strong or woody ornamentals. They grow in most soils and under most conditions (out of direct sunlight, however) ; but they do best when planted in a compost of 2 parts loam and 1 part of a mixture of dried cow manure, crumbled old mortar (always available where a house is being razed) , and sand. Water moderately when resting, freely when plants are making growth. Overhead baskets of these shed seed freely, so watch for seedlings in containers of plants growing below. Division is the common method of propagation. All are easy to grow from seed.

Episcia   Flame-violet   Gesneriad Family
    These are excellent pendent plants for a partly sunny window in a rather cool room. Mine grow on glass shelves in the breakfast room, and the colorful foliage is prettier than many flowers. Humidity is critical; don't try them unless you can guarantee a minimum humidity of 30 percent—higher is even better. The potting compost is equal

parts loam, leafmold, brown peat, and ½ part perlite or sand. I prefer the perlite as it seems to stabilize the moisture content of the medium. Hanging baskets are best, but pots on brackets will suffice. All these should be near the glass. Water only enough to keep the soil barely damp; in winter, allow to go slightly dry before rewatering. Apply dilute fish emulsion solution once a month or more frequently when plants are in vigorous growth. Most episcias propagate readily from cuttings rooted in perlite and peat under a plastic cover. Outstanding as a flowering plant is the species *E. dianthiflora* with tubular white flowers heavily fringed at the edge. But the real show comes from the cultivars with metallic foliage: bronze, silver, chocolate, and old gold. The pink, green, and bronze variegated sorts, too, are quite fine. Probably derived largely from *E. fulgida,* most of these were random-hybridized by African-violet enthusiasts, with little or no control of breeding stocks, so that parentage is largely a matter of speculation.

Ferns are satisfactory basket plants and are useful in pots on window brackets or in plant stands where the fronds can spread downward. The left photo shows a young plant of *Nephrolepis exaltata,* with its very fine but tough leaves. The right photo is a *Davallia.* Note the attractive furry rhizomes creeping from the pot.

Ferns

All ferns that grow well indoors thrive in hanging baskets, though the large, upright ones look quite out of place in them. While a well-mossed basket makes a satisfactory container for ferns, I prefer to line the basket with osmunda fiber (orchid fiber) sliced into very thin sheets. Often the ferns grow right through, or rhizomes creep out of the top of the basket and downward, clinging closely to the damp fiber. The result is a dense cluster of fern fronds—healthy and handsome. While it is possible to find highly specialized soil mixtures for each genus of fern, I find that a general mix suits most kinds very well. Try equal parts loam, brown peat,

Staghorn ferns are among the boldest plants available for indoor growing. True epiphytes, growing with their roots in the fibrous bark of a tree, these are best handled by fastening the plant to a block of orchid fiber. Fern and block may be set in an ornamental container, as shown, but the fern will do best when simply suspended with free air circulation around the base.

leafmold, and old dried manure, with ½ part each sand and crushed hardwood charcoal added.

Ferns respond well to humidity; they suffer from overwatering. Keep the substrate damp always, but never wet. Syringe the foliage often. In summer step up watering somewhat and, when new fronds are coming on, add a trace of fish emulsion to the water. These ferns will all do well at cool room temperature in good light but out of direct sun: *Adiantum,* the maidenhair ferns; *Davallia,* ball fern, rabbit's-foot fern and others; *Drynaria* (no common name for these ferns with heavy, creeping rhizomes); *Nephrolepis,* including the Boston fern and its many forms; *Polypodium,* a large, diverse group, many of which are good basket subjects, including the common polypody fern; and *Pteris,* the brake and table ferns of the tropics, suitable, in many cases, for huge baskets bearing decumbent fronds drooping 3 feet or more. Some of the group are much smaller.

Staghorn ferns, *Platycerium* species, are a special case. Wire a plate of osmunda to a wooden block; lay the fern roots on this, cover with damp sphagnum, and wire in place. Hang the fern in a bright or partly sunny place. High humidity is essential.

Ficus   Ornamental Fig   Mulberry Family
Two of the climbing figs, *Ficus pumila* (*F. repens*) and its several varieties and *F. sarmentosa,* make suitable basket plants. Rather difficult in the home, as they want diffuse light, steady warmth, and extreme humidity, they do reasonably well in plant rooms and garden greenhouses. I have seen fine baskets of both of these in gardens along the Gulf of Mexico. Both have creeping stems any tiny leaves that overlap. Properly trained, these quickly clothe a hanging basket. A suitable compost is 3 parts loam, 1 part each peat and sand. Water moderately through winter months, freely the remainder of the year. Apply dilute liquid organic fertilizer sparingly as ficus is sensitive to a build-up of minerals in the soil.

Geraniums   See page 74.

Gesneriads
Several genera of the African-violet family include species that trail or produces offsets on trailing runners. All of these make wonderful basket or shelf plants, but few are suited to the average home as they demand very high humidity.

Among those that tolerate average house conditions are the episcias, some of the columneas and hypocyrtas. Pot these in equal parts fibrous loam, peat, leafmold, and ½ part sand or perlite. Keep them moderately damp, in strong light but not necessarily direct sunlight, and they will make full, healthy plants.

The hypocyrtas are relatively new to the American market; at least five species, *H. nummularia, H. selloana, H. strigillosa, H. teuscheri,* and *H. wettsteinii* are available. All make basket subjects for window culture; the last is probably the most ornamental. Recently promoted by a mail-order company that creates its own common names, it was listed as "goldfish plant," a name with no official standing. This plant produces long flexuous greenish stems well furnished with shiny, curved, green leaves in pairs. From the axils of the leaves come tubular red-orange flowers with a lower pouch and a golden-yellow mouth. The plant is beautiful both in bloom and just in foliage. It responds to the same care that produces fine saint-paulias.

Propagate all trailing members of the gesneriad group by rooting short lengths of stem in a peat-perlite mixture under a plastic cover. Or pot up offset plants of episcia in the appropriate compost and keep in a draft-free place until established.

Helxine Baby's-tears   Nettle Family

This fragile-appearing miniature trailing plant is tough and reliable. It is ideal for a tiny hanging pot or basket. It makes a fine edging for outdoor baskets, boxes, and urns in shady sites. Grow it in equal parts loam, peat, and sand. Water only to keep barely damp, and apply very dilute organic fertilizer solution at long intervals through summer. The species is *H. solierolli;* growing only 2 to 3 inches high, it spreads rapidly over bare soil. Propagate by division.

With a little encouragement, baby's-tears can be made to grow on the outside of a mossed basket—especially desirable when dead sphagnum or sheet moss would otherwise be seen from within.

Hoya Wax-flower   Milkweed Family

New kinds of this interesting house plant appear on the market from time to time. All are strictly house plants, and most may be trained in pendent fashion, especially when grown in a hanging pot or basket. The best compost is equal parts peat and loam with some sand and bits of hardwood charcoal added. Grow these in full sunlight; average temperature suffices, though *H. bella* likes it really hot and humid. Water freely March through September, moderately October to March. Apply any liquid fertilizer solution monthly through the summer. Do not prune away spent flower stalks as they often produce a second crop of flowers.

Propagate all kinds by taking three-joint-long cuttings of year-old shoots in late March. Remove the lowest pair of leaves, dip the stalk in rooting hormone, and stick in a mixture of equal parts peat and sand in a clean pot under a clear plastic cover. Hold at about 80° F. until rooted.

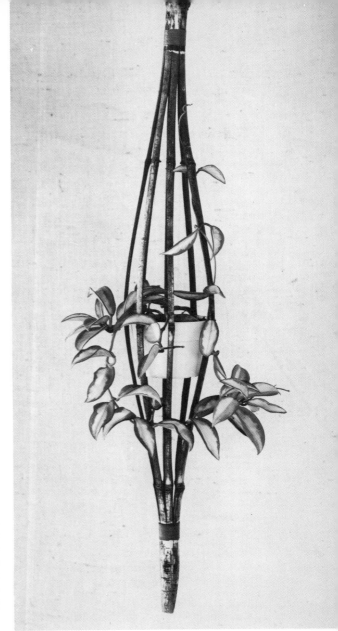

The hoyas are exotic plants, blooming or just in leaf; this hanging arrangement consists of an inch-diameter piece of bamboo, split lengthwise and forced apart to allow the insertion of a 4-inch pot of *Hoya exotica*.

Kinds commonly available include *H. carnosa* (with several varieties), *H. bella, H. purpureo-fusca* 'Silver Pink', and *H. motoskei*. Several upright species have appeared on the retail market in recent years, but these do not adapt to pendent growth.

Ipomoea   Sweet Potato; Morning-glory   Morning-glory Family

Everybody's first hanging plant is a sweet potato. Select a tuber with active eyes (today freshly dug tubers are chemically treated to retard sprouting, but the chemical gradually wears away and eventually buds become active) and set it, root-end down, in a glass or jar of water. The end with eyes should be halfway out of the water. Grow in a sunny window, average room temperature, and let nature take its course. If you pinch the shoots frequently while young, you will have a bushier plant. Various specialists have tried to introduce selections of sweet potato with exceptionally ornamental foliage for house-plant growing, but these never have caught on. By all means, start all the neighborhood children on sweet-potato growing during the late winter months; you may discover another Burbank.

Oriental strains of morning-glory offered by American seedsmen as 'Imperial Giant Fringed' and 'Japanese Imperial' make fine basket plants for early-spring indoor growing and for later in the garden. File the hard seeds or soak overnight; plant two or three to a pot and bring the seedlings on under lights or on the window sill of a cool room. Prepare a heavily mossed basket, fill with equal parts loam, peat, and sand, and set in three seedlings. Pinch plants frequently to make them bushy, then let them trail. As buds start, push with liquid fertilizer weekly and keep the soil evenly moist. The 6-inch cerise, rose, blue, or purple blossoms are astonishing. Fun for the sunny plant room, these are a knockout in the garden.

Kalanchoe   Stonecrop Family

Most readily available members of this succulent-leaved group of plants may be basket grown, and with age decumbent branches will develop. A well-planted basket of the familiar Christmas kalanchoe is hard to beat. All want average room temperature, humidity as high as possible, full sunlight, and a chance to dry slightly between waterings. Most grow well in equal parts loam, peat, and sand. Apply ½ strength liquid fertilizer monthly from late spring until blooms begin to open.

A unique species is *K. uniflora,* an epiphytic creeper from Madagascar. Grow this trailing sort in fir bark or osmunda fiber, orchid-fashion, and include a trace of fish emulsion solution in every watering. Possible for a warm window, this crimson-flowered species is more luxuriant in a warm plant room or greenhouse.

Lotus   Legume Family
    See under Tender Woody Plants, Chapter 6.

Mahernia Honeybells   Chocolate Family
    This newcomer to home flower growing makes a perfect hanging-basket plant. The species known as honeybells is *M. verticillata* and comes from South Africa. Grow it at average room temperature in a bright, sunny window. Humidity may be a problem, as this plant requires at least 30 percent. The soil mixture is 1 part each loam, sand, leafmold, and 2 parts damp brown peat. Pot up in a basket, and when growth resumes keep evenly damp. Apply dilute liquid fertilizer from September until bloom fails in the spring. This winter-blooming, woody little plant bears fernlike foliage on rambling, drooping branches. The ¾-inch-long bell-shaped yellow flowers bob happily, and they emit a pervading fragrance.

Manettia   Madder Family
    M. bicolor is the only commonly available member of this group of climbing South American plants. Pot up in equal parts loam, peat, and sand, with crushed hardwood charcoal added. Water freely through warm weather, sparingly at other times. Syringe daily when growth is active. These enjoy average room temperature only as long as the humidity is quite high; if the plant sulks, move to a cooler room. Grow in bright light, little direct sun. Propagation is said to be possible by seed or cuttings; I recommend buying small plants from a specialist.
    Pruning is a great part of success when growing *M. bicolor*. Train the vine out and down from a bracket-supported pot. Cut back sharply after flowering, and when growth resumes, pinch frequently until buds start to form. This is a wonderful plant for the home greenhouse or plant room.

Maranta   (see also *Calathea*)   Arrowroot Family
    Marantas are relatives of the plant that produces arrowroot. The

small, ornamental species, *M. bicolor* and *M. leuconeura* with its varieties *kerchoveana* (leaves spotted red), and *M. massangeana* (leaves purplish beneath) make fine pot plants. When basket grown, eventually crowded plants droop outward and downward, producing a lush tropical effect. These thrive in average home conditions if the humidity is reasonably high. Average window light is satisfactory. Grow in a compost of equal parts loam, leafmold, and peat, with ½ part each sand and crushed hardwood charcoal added. Water copiously through warm weather, moderately through fall and early winter, and grow nearly dry from midwinter until March. Repot annually; if plants fail to multiply, increase peat content of the potting mixture and increase feeding. These normally require only two or three modest feedings of liquid manure through the summer. They are propagated by dividing at repotting time in March.

Though tender house plants, these make fine pot or urn plants for the shady summer garden.

Orchids   Orchid Family

Any of the epiphytic orchids (those that perch on trees above ground rather than growing with their roots in soil) may be basket grown, and some make quite acceptable specimens, though with orchids the beauty lies in the blossom, not the plant.

But no orchid is enthusiastic about house conditions. The light is too one-sided and usually too dim. The humidity is intolerably low. The air is stale, drafty, too hot or too cold. If you have a warm plant room, try baskets of *Phalaenopsis* or other warm-room sorts. If you have a moderately cool plant room or greenhouse where the humidity is kept high, try the *Cattleya* hybrids. Orchids are great fun, very undemanding (in the right environment) and quite floriferous if you meet their basic needs. I grow all of mine in baskets in the greenhouse so I do not have to watch so carefully for overwatering, because the light is stronger there and ventilation is better.

Oxalis Wood Sorrel   Wood-sorrel Family

Given a cool room (65° F. or below), a bright sunny window, with the humidity as high as possible, you can enjoy the innocent beauty of oxalis baskets month after month. The foliage is handsome,

The Bermuda-buttercup is really an oxalis; these small cormacious plants are perfect for a little basket in the window. Various species come in white, pink, red, or yellow. Cram a number of bulbs into your container to obtain the fullest possible display.

like large 3- or 4-leaved clovers. The clusters of small, funnel-shaped flowers are pure Pollyanna. Some are herbaceous perennials, other are bulbous-rooted. Autumn-, winter-, and spring-flowering kinds are for the house, plant room, and greenhouse. Summer types are charming, suspended from the shade tree over a terrace tea table. The compost is sandy loam; equal parts loam, peat, and sand make a fine mixture too. Pot up as follows: autumn-flowering, August; winter-flowering, September and October; spring-flowering, January and February; summer-flowering, March or April. After potting up oxalis, place in a warmish window and water sparingly until growth is active, then water freely; move to a cool place when growth is strong. Bulbous kinds are best potted up ½ dozen per 5- or 6-inch basket or pot; set them ½ inch deep and ½ inch apart. When buds appear, feed weekly with very dilute liquid fertilizer; discontinue when blooms become sparse. As the last flowers fade, gradually withhold water and keep perennial sorts barely going, bulbous kinds quite dry, until you want to start growth again. Repot annually.

Some of the best are: Autumn-flowering, *O. carnosa,* yellow; *O. variabilis,* red, white, or pink; and *O. bowieana,* pink. Winter-flowering, *O. braziliensis,* rosy-red; *O. incarnata,* white, tinged pink; and *O. purpurea,* rose. Spring-flowering, *O. pes-caprae* (*O. cernua*), yellow (this is the Bermuda-buttercup); *O. rosea,* rose; *O. rubra,* rose with red veins. Summer-flowering, *O hirta,* red; *O. tetraphylla,* red; *O floribunda,* rose; and *O. deppei,* red. There are many more kinds available in the trade, including hardy garden sorts.

Passiflora   Passion-flower   Passion-flower Family

Most passifloras may be basket-grown if pruned frequently. They are too rampant for box and urn culture though sometimes used. The potting compost is equal parts loam and peat, with $\frac{1}{4}$ part fine sand added. Grow these hot, up to 75° F., for best blossoming, though they may be overwintered at 55° F., if no winter bloom is desired. Water copiously March to September and moderately October to March. Spray the foliage daily through the blooming period. While buds are forming, apply *very* dilute organic fertilizer solution biweekly. Prune out all weak shoots as they are produced and from time to time cut back vigorous shoots strongly. Twine the vines around the rim of the basket as they form. Six-inch shoots of these will root in sandy soil under a plastic cover through summer.

The truly tropical kinds suitable for basket growing include *P. alata,* crimson; *P. edulis,* white and purple; *P. racemosa,* red, white, and purple; and others.

Warm-climate kinds include: *P. mixta,* pink; *P. mollissima,* rose; and *P. caerulea,* purple, pink, or white. Select varieties of the last are available.

Pellionia   Nettle Family

These rather uncommon creeping tropicals make nice pot plants for growing on window brackets where the stems spill over the containers and droop gracefully. The potting compost is 1 part each

Pellionia daveauana is related to baby's-tears and artillery plant; with beautifully marked foliage, this plant needs the warmth and humidity of a conservatory or plant room. It sometimes is used in sheltered patio gardens in the deep South.

loam, leafmold, and peat, and 2 parts sand. Average room temperature is suitable for most species; grow near a north window or in other rather dim light. These require only moderate watering in winter—do not let the container dry deeply—but they should be freely watered during warm months. Division in spring is the easiest way to propagate; cuttings of creeping shoots, inserted in sandy soil under a plastic cover at 80° F., usually root. If stems fail to develop nice

Peperomia scandens as it grows under optimum conditions in the tropical greenhouse. In the home window the plant is smaller, less vigorous, but no less graceful and beautiful, throughout the year.

color, give more light. These seldom require fertilizer; but if plants lag, give very dilute, organic, liquid fertilizer. Available species include *P. daveauana* and *P. pulchra.*

Peperomia   Pepper Family

Peperomias with creeping or decumbent stems are natural candidates for hanging-basket culture. Some can be dibbled into the sides of a basket where they develop into quite nice specimens. The recommended compost is equal parts loam, peat, and sand, though in a basket, with all-round drainage, ½ part sand suffices, or may be replaced with perlite to stabilize the moisture content of the mixture. Grow these in bright light, out of direct sunlight; they appreciate warmth and high humidity. If leaves show marginal drying, move to a cooler, more humid location. Water generously, then allow to dry only slightly before rewatering. Syringe the plants throughout warm weather; feed only rarely with liquid house-plant fertilizer. Cuttings taken in summer and stuck in a mixture of equal parts peat and perlite usually root quickly. Handsome plants for basket culture include *P. prostrata, P. fosteriana,* and *P. cubensis.* There are many more. I like to grow the dime-store kind, *P. obtusifolia,* and its several handsome varieties, in squatty pots on window brackets. The fleshy stems hang down, showing the leaves to great advantage.

Philodendron   Arum Family

Dozens of species, varieties, and cultivars of *Philodendron* are offered for home use. But they should not be, as few homes offer the extremely high humidity demanded. A viny one, *P. micans,* with leaves that are silky-bronze above, reddish beneath, makes a fair basket plant in a bright, sun-free window of a relatively cool, humid room. I grow it quite successfully in the kitchen and bathroom windows. Use a wire basket, heavily mossed and filled with a compost of equal parts loam, leafmold, peat, and rather fine sand. Water freely the year round, syringe daily with tepid water. Use plastic hairpins to secure stems to the outside of the basket, where they will eventually root. Give liquid house-plant fertilizer monthly. Propagate by rooting shoots in water or damp perlite, or by layering on the surface of a basket.

In the warm home greenhouse or plant room most vining-type philodendrons grow enthusiastically. Planted in baskets or in boxes on high brackets, these can be trained downward to make beautiful cascades of handsome foliage. Many will produce odd calla-like blossoms in late winter.

Pilea   Nettle Family

This diverse group of plants includes several that are suitable for basket plantings. The two low, spreading kinds are quite dissimilar; *P. depressa* is succulent, with tiny roundish shiny pea-green leaves on thin green stems that root freely at the nodes. *P. repens,* the black panamiga plant, bears smallish rounded quilted leaves with notched edges; the foliage of this is glossy copper-brown above and purplish and hairy beneath. The stems are hairy and brown. Both are quite handsome grown as specimens or when used in group plantings. A third sort, the artillery plant, *P. microphylla,* sometimes is used in baskets as a filler, but surely other, more desirable, plants are available. The aluminum plant, *P. cadierei,* is another relative, but unsuitable for decumbent growing.

The potting compost for all pileas is equal parts loam, leafmold or brown peat, and sand. Grow at cool-room temperature over winter, humidity as high as possible; keep plants in bright light but not in direct sunlight. Water freely through hot weather, moderately in winter. Apply dilute liquid manure or fish emulsion solution monthly, March through July. Propagate by taking 3-inch cuttings in summer; root in a perlite-peat mixture under a plastic cover.

Plectranthus   Swedish-ivy   Mint Family

All plectranthus species and varieties make good trailing house plants; they also do well when moved to the garden over the summer. A suitable compost is 2 parts loam, 1 part each of peat and sand. Grow near a window in a moderately cool room (the cooler the better, but these tolerate average conditions), with the humidity as high as possible. Keep evenly moist and water copiously during hot summer days. When growing these in the garden, hose off the plants daily. Fertilize with liquid manure not more than once each month. These do very well over the winter on a cool sun porch where usually they bloom freely.

There is considerable confusion about common names here. The familiar plant with fresh green, waxy, leaves is *P. australis.* Its flowers are white or nearly white. This is the plant that is usually called Swedish-ivy, though the sort seen in most Swedish homes is *P. oertendahlii.* This species bears green-to-bronze leaves, slightly hairy above and purplish below, with a handsome network of light-colored veins. Flower sprays are pale pink. One of the handsomest of basket plants is its variety *P. oertendahlii* var. *variegatus,* with milk-white leaf margins and blotches. Other kinds worth growing are *P. ciliatus* and *P. purpuratus,* both of smaller proportions than the above species.

Schizocentron   Meadow-beauty Family

This handsome native of Mexico has recently made a comeback. No one heard of Spanish shawl, *S. elegans,* until a few years ago, and now several dealers handle it. The plant is smallish, of creeping habit, forming a dense mat of reddish stems that root at the nodes. The ½-inch-long, ovate leaves are dark green and slightly hairy. Through summer, this plant often is completely covered with small purplish-rose flowers. It is a fine basket plant for the plant room, home greenhouse, and Southern patio garden. Difficult in the house because it demands high humidity, it can be grown in a bathroom or kitchen window away from direct sunlight.

The potting compost is equal parts loam, peat, leafmold and fine sand. Water freely March through September, moderately (never allowing plant to become dry) the rest of the year. Fertilize with very dilute liquid organic fertilizer spring through late summer. *S. elegans* is best propagated by sticking young shoots in a perlite-peat mixture under a plastic cover. Bottom heat is almost essential. In the house, set pots or boxes on a warm (not hot) radiator; in the greenhouse, on benches warmed by the pipes.

As this plant roots at the nodes, you can peg down the trailing stems, using plastic hairpins to hold them close to the mossed sides of a basket. In this way it is quite possible to root the plant entirely over the underside of a hanging basket.

Scindapsus   Devil's-ivy, Pothos   Arum Family

This is the plant florist's sell as pothos. It resembles a philodendron, but, unlike philodendrons, this thrives in average house conditions. Pot in a mixture of equal parts loam, coarse brown peat, chopped sphagnum moss, and coarse sand with a bit of charcoal added to cope with minerals in city water. Grow near a window or under a light that burns for at least 10 hours daily. Water moderately through cold weather, freely other times. *Scindapsus* looks best when syringed frequently; fertilize only occasionally with any soluble house-plant fertilizer.

The most common sort is *S. aureus* with elongated heart-shaped leaves, medium green with yellow variegations. A more attractive sort is its cultivar 'Marble Queen', with almost entirely variegated or white leaves. Lacking chlorophyll, it is touchy, resenting chill, wet feet, or too-dim light. There are other good cultivars. My favorite of all the philodendron-like group is *S. pictus argyraeus*. The overlapping cordate leaves are a satiny bluish-green, dark, with rhomboidal splotches of silver-green spaced sparsely over the surface. Grow in a pot from which the plant can trail or, better, in a basket, and peg the stems loosely to the moss with hairpins. Remember to turn the basket occasionally so the plant can develop evenly. To propagate, root 6-inch cuttings in a potting mix under a plastic cover.

Sedum   Stonecrop Family

Two sedums make excellent pendent plants for the house; they are *S. caeruleum,* an annual, easily grown from seed for its late-summer blue flowers (this is also a fine urn or box plant) , and *S. morganianum,* a tender Mexican perennial, quite decumbent, with ropes of closely placed, translucent yellow-green leaves (spindle-shaped) with a blue sheen. The rarely produced terminal flowers are light pink. This plant commonly is called the burro's-tail sedum.

The potting compost is equal parts loam, sand, small brick rubble or finely broken crocks, and dried cow manure. Grow in full sun, at average room temperature. Water freely from April through September, then grow very dry. *S morganianum* roots quickly when stems are stuck in sandy soil. As an experiment, moss and fill a basket, then cover the soil with plastic, invert the basket, and sparsely sprinkle seed of *S. caeruleum* over the moss. When the sedum begins to bud, turn the basket right side up again and plant it with any handy bushy flower. The sedum will completely cover the bottom and sides of the basket and will bloom beautifully.

Selaginella Club-moss   Club-moss Family

These plants, resembling large moss plants (they are relatives of the true mosses) , make wonderful basket and box plants. But they

From seed, *Sedum coeruleum*, a heavy-flowering annual plant, makes a bright display in just a few weeks. Fine for boxes and urns, it also may be grown in a basket, or you may sow seed on the moss of an inverted basket, wait for it to develop somewhat, then hang the basket right side up and plant it with an additional plant.

are not for the average home. Some are tropical, demanding a steamy environment; others are from the temperate-zone bogs, and they, too, want extreme humidity, though lower temperatures. The potting mixture is equal parts coarse brown peat, pulled apart into fibrous bunches, and chopped, fresh sphagnum moss. These are grown in shade, with moderate light; water copiously April to September, moderately afterwards. Plants should be syringed daily while in active growth. Little if any fertilizer is necessary, though *very* dilute liquid manure or fish emulsion sometimes brightens the color. Propagate by division or by cuttings rooted in potting mix under a close environment.

A hanging basket well filled with one or several kinds of selanginella is a thing of great beauty. In the conservatory or plant room use the creeping and climbing sorts to edge shelves and boxes. You will have beautiful green lace trailing below your upright plants.

Senecio   German-ivy, Parlor-ivy   Daisy Family
    It is tempting to list a number of the southern hemisphere senecios as they are interesting to grow, unusual in appearance, and some thrive in a hanging container. But, alas, they are almost impossible to find. Watch for unusual hanging plants in this genus while visiting the tropical houses of botanic gardens; maybe the keeper will give you a small plant from his stock bench.
    German-ivy is *S. mikanioides.* This is another of those house plants that thrives when all else fails. With fresh green ivy-shaped lobed leaves and a twining habit, it grows well on a pedestal or hanging from a basket. The compost is equal parts loam, peat, and sand. Water to keep barely moist; add fertilizer to the water monthly through warm weather. Grow near a window, out of direct sunlight. The cooler the room, the better the plant. Given a little midwinter sun, sometimes this produces fragrant yellow daisylike flowers. Propagate by rooting cuttings in perlite-peat mix in a warm, enclosed place. A few small pots of German-ivy are a great addition to a window-sill collection and handy to move to the living room when guests are expected.
    S. confusus, with leaves similar to German-ivy but more arrow-shaped, is a nice window-sill trailer when you can find it. The small orange-red florets are welcome in midwinter. Grow it like German-ivy.

Smilax
    The shiny-leaved smilax of florists is *Asparagus asparagoides,* described earlier in this chapter.

Streptosolen   Orange-browallia   Nightshade Family
    This handsome basket plant once was classified as a *Browallia*

species. Today it is called *Streptosolen jamesonii*. A handsome house plant the year round, baskets of blooming plants are a great addition to the summer garden too. The potting compost is equal parts loam, brown peat, and sand. Grow this in a high humidity, average room temperature, right in a sunny window. Plant-room or greenhouse conditions are much better. Water freely April to October, only moderately during winter. Add liquid fertilizers to the water biweekly during warm weather. Prune severely after flowering is over. In the garden, protect from direct sunlight. Cuttings taken in late spring root readily in a mixture of equal parts sand and damp peat. The container should be covered with a plastic cover or glass bell.

Try a basket of this—one plant per 12-inch basket—with baby's-tears or *Sedum caeruleum* in the moss and around the base of the plant.

Syngonium   Arum Family

Two species of these calla-lily relatives are valuable for hanging baskets. One, *S. erythrophyllum,* is difficult to find, though specialists in Florida sometimes stock it. Its creeping rhizomes carry arrow-shaped waxy leaves, coppery green, with tiny pink dots. This is an excellent plant for growing on the *outside* of a basket. The more familiar syngonium is *S. podophyllum,* with numerous varieties and cultivars. Florists' shops usually list it as nephthytis. Fifteen-inch-high leaves rise from a creeping rootstock. Young leaves are arrow-shaped, older ones are trifoliate. *This is one of the most indestructible house plants.* It grows under almost any conditions, as long as the soil never dries completely and it gets sufficient light to keep the foliage from turning lemon-yellow. While it does not "hang" when pot grown, if planted in a basket, it will spill over the edge and grow down over the moss. Many of the selected strains have colorful foliage resembling the caladium.

The potting compost is equal parts loam, peat, and sand. Apply any liquid house-plant fertilizer at monthly intervals. Keep moderately damp, never dry, never soggy. Given a warm, steamy environment with moderately bright light, these become unbelievably luxuriant.

The spiderwort relatives that trail all make up into durable pendent plants for growing indoors. And they can be moved to the garden over summer to cut down on inside work. Some of the most colorful and useful ones are shown in this illustration.

The zebra-plant, *Zebrina pendula,* develops into a voluminous specimen when kept in a conservatory, as the photo shows. One or two sprigs growing in a small ornamental bottle (it will grow in water alone for many months) make a good window-sill decoration. Or pot up in a basket and grow it indoors or out.

Tradescantia   (Including *Callisia, Setcreasea, Tripogandra, Zebrina*)   Wandering Jew, Zebra-plant   Spiderwort Family
    These are brittle, soft-stemmed, pendent plants with rather linear leaves that clasp the stem. Flowers are 3-petaled and silky, usually blue, pink, or white, and short-lived. Inclined to be rather weedy, tradescantias make good filler plants for baskets. They take average room conditions. Grow near a window in or out of sun, keep

evenly moist, and fertilize frequently during warm weather, not at all in winter. Syringe daily in summer. My choice of these are the variegated types, such as, *Callisia elegans, Setcreasea pallida, Zebrina pendula discolor, Tradescantia fluminensis variegata* and *T. albiflora laekenensis.* I find them tolerable as house plants, and wonderful to use at the edges of boxes, tubs, and urns in the summer garden. A few plants carried over in the window supply cuttings to root in perlite and peat mixture for summer use. Amenable to any soil, equal parts of loam, peat, and sand suffice for indoor growing.

A very special cousin to these, once classified as *Tradescantia,* is a favorite of mine. It is *Tripogandra multiflora.* With hairlike wiry purple stems and less-than-inch-long leaves, this miniature makes a perfect hanging-basket specimen in a 4-inch container. When the airy sprays of ¼-inch white flowers are borne on almost invisible pedicels, the result is charming.

4

For Terrace and Garden

Petunias, alyssum, lobelia, and ivy-geraniums cascade down the sides of pots and urns on the terrace, bringing the garden up onto the pavement. Tuberous begonias, fuchsias, and various foliage plants trail down from overhead hanging baskets. Pendent house plants, upright standards, and kinds in hanging containers move to the garden for the summer. Certain environmental conditions favor all these plants.

The greatest enemy of hanging plants is wind. Wind tears at basket-grown begonias and fuchsias, shattering the blossoms and shriveling the foliage. Wind tangles the pendent branches of the weeping standard rose and knots or twists the delicate trailers of variegated vinca spilling out of the window box. When you are strolling through the garden, looking for places to use baskets, urns, and boxes effectively, keep in mind shelter from wind.

Light is required by all green plants; some want direct sunlight; others prefer the diffuse rays of light filtering through a high old tree; still others want the perpetual shadow of a house. But every plant needs light; a plant may grow in the shade, but it won't grow in the dark. A basket hung under the eaves of the house must be turned frequently. The entire basket is in shadow, but the side nearest the house also is in the dark. Be sure you know the light needs of your plants before you place them. For example, impatiens must have shade, or at most, dappled sunlight, while lantana deteriorates quickly in anything less than dawn-to-sunset sunlight.

All of this business of wind-shelter and proper light control brings up an interesting point. Hanging-basket plants, urn plants, standards, in many cases, want to live close to the house. They are part of the family as no perennial border or rose-garden specimen can be. They depend on you for the correct placement—and for daily care.

PLANTS FOR VARIOUS ENVIRONMENTS

Basket-grown summer annuals—including plants that are treated as annuals, such as begonias, geraniums (pelargoniums), and other non-woody kinds—want the same light conditions they enjoy in the open garden, but with more shelter from wind. A large basket planted to balcony-type petunias makes a marvelous feature for east-facing entryway eaves. Petunias, lantanas, geraniums, coleus, cape plumbago, variegated *Vinca major,* trailing nasturtiums, and other familiar plants thrive in window boxes on the south and east sides of the house, provided they are not shaded by trees or nearby buildings. The north and shaded west exposures call for impatiens, tuberous begonias, fibrous-rooted begonias, impatiens, creeping periwinkle, and browallia. A good rule of thumb, when assembling garden annuals for basket, urn, or box, is to follow the requirements of the plant in the garden. If it grows best in the sun when bedded out, put it in the basket that is to brighten a sunny place. If it blooms best in a shady bed, plant it with other shade-lovers in whatever container you are using.

House plants and tender woody species moved to the garden for summer growth and color require somewhat more careful manipulation. While the basket of *Lotus berthelotii* or the large hanging pot of *Hypocyrta wettsteinii* may take the sunniest window in the house or conservatory, either may sunscald badly when exposed to direct sunlight outdoors. In fact, all house plants require careful hardening off when moved outside to the harsher air and brighter light of the open garden. Always give them—even the sun-lovers—a few days in bright shade, followed by a few days in dappled sunlight, before trying them in full sun. And watch for signs of sunscald; at the first indication of discoloration on the leaves—bronzing, bleaching, or yellowing—move the plant to dimmer light for a few days. And, of course, full protection from wind is very important for the first few days.

"The herb lady," Katherine Williams, taught me years ago about the "little by little" method for bringing plants out into the garden and moving them back into the house in the fall. If you have ever lived in India, you will recognize it as a variation of the technique servants use to "annex" a valuable box or other table ornament. They don't just take it—but day by day it moves from table to table, leaving the living room for the hallway, to be wafted from thence into the servants' quarters, and from there it is seen no more. When house plants are to go out, first move them inside to a bright window and open the sash to give them the feel of fresh air. After a couple of days, move them just outside the door, into full shade and shelter. From there they go into the dappled light under the big oak tree. And finally, hardened off, with all foliage intact, they are planted in the terrace urns or their baskets are hung overhead in bright light.

Plants are even touchier about leaving the humid, bright, cool autumn garden to go into the hot, dry air and dimmer light of the house. Move them first into light shade for a few days. Then onto the porch where the light is even dimmer, and dew does not bathe their leaves. After a few more days, move them inside, to your brightest, coolest window, and spray the foliage with a mist of tepid water each morning. Probably you can preserve all the lush summer foliage and new shoots.

GEOGRAPHY MAKES A DIFFERENCE

Plants behave differently in various geographic areas, and the difference is especially noticeable with basket and box-grown plants because the root system is somewhat stressed by the changes in temperature. For example, *Lotus berthelotii* makes a silvery-gray cloud of fine foliage on pendent branches in a sunny Montana garden, and bears a crop of great, claw-shaped, hot orange, chocolate striped flowers. In a basket in Kansas City it does not bloom at all, and the plant may deteriorate rapidly if subjected to any wind. The humidity and high temperatures of much of the Middle West are just too much for this species. But it makes a fine conservatory plant throughout the country. In Vancouver, Minneapolis, Rochester, and Bangor, lobelias produce long trailers of glistening foliage almost hidden by always-present flowers. The same cultivars, grown south of the Mason-Dixon line—or its equivalent stretched from the Atlantic to the Pacific—may sunscald badly in the open, but make ideal basket, box, and urn specimens in semishade. You learn these things by experience and by visiting local botanic gardens and arboreta.

Soil usually is not much of a problem with basket and box plants. Use a basic mixture, quite porous, with plenty of drainage at the bottom of the container, and most of your plants will thrive. But some species are more particular, and concessions are required. For example, one widely used soil mix for tuberous begonias consists of equal parts of well-rotted cow manure, leafmold, garden loam, brown peat, and fine sand. This is a high-humus medium that is about neutral as regards acidity. For fuchsias, one specialist recommends a mixture of composted loam, leafmold, and a little sand, with a dusting of wood ash. Details of these special media are given in Chapter 8.

CHOOSING YOUR CONTAINERS

Numerous factors enter into the choice of basket, urn, or window box. Practicality, durability, appropriateness, pleasing appearance—these and more must be considered. But the demands of the plants come first. Each plant needs a certain amount of root space, and that will dictate size. Each plant needs adequate drainage, so that eliminates containers lacking drain holes. A plant needs a reasonably cool root run, and that eliminates metal boxes and urns—as well as some plastics.

With window boxes, usually the house style determines the

material from which the box is to be made, how it is to be finished, and what its lines are to be. Customarily the box more or less duplicates the lines and style of the window sills. After all, the point is not to feature the box. The plants are the thing. The box is just a necessary adjunct, and should not stand out. Minimum dimensions of a window box in cross section are 6 inches deep and 6 inches wide; 8 by 8 inches is better. Too large a box and the weight of the required soil make it difficult to prevent sides from bulging and to provide adquate support. Too shallow a box does not allow for depth of roots. Drill drain holes every 6 inches across the bottom of the box in a scattered pattern. Boxes made of 1-inch-thick cypress or redwood and put together with brass or aluminum screws will wear for a long time.

I have a thing about the suitability of urns, and frequently am at odds with people who like urns of contemporary design. To me a garden urn should be purely functional and quite plain unless it is in a rigidly formal garden, and then it should be a classic marble vase. For the informal garden terrace, or on a low wall or the rim of a pool, clean, hard-fired terra-cotta flowerpots are hard to beat. Their porosity keeps roots aerated and rather cool. They are modest and do not detract from the garden or from the plants growing in them. And they are relatively inexpensive and durable. Right away I must eat my words about not liking contemporary designs because the Keller Company has come out with a contemporary design of a terra-cotta pot that is superbly formed and fired of first-quality clay. If you live in a mansion and decorate your garden with Georgian urns of wrought lead, think of slipping a pot or even a plastic or tarpaper liner into the opening rather than subjecting your valuable antique to the corrosive action of soil.

POTTING AND WATERING

If a plant has special requirements, as indicated for tuberous begonias and fuchsias, do your best to make the growing medium right so your plant can do its utmost. Otherwise, use the good old mixture of equal parts garden loam, damp brown peat, and coarse sand, with a handful of bonemeal added to each bushel of mixture. When plants go to the garden in spring, repot them if they need it; otherwise, with a knife scrape an inch or two of soil from the top of the container—basket, pot, or urn—and replace it with the appropriate mixture. I have a special technique for this; the replacement soil is always equal parts well-rotted barnyard manure and river sand. But not everybody can get barnyard manure, so the loam-peat-sand mixture is used. Most of my basket plants are discarded each fall after cuttings are taken and stuck in perlite in the little greenhouse or under lights in the basement. I save no more than one specimen of each kind, as there just isn't room.

As the cuttings root, they are potted up, first in 3-inch pots, and then moved on as necessary. By spring most are in 4- or 5-inch pots and, having been pinched, are of respectable size. These plants are ideal for baskets and urns, as they are of vigorous young wood with lots of buds. After a short time to acclimatize in the garden, they are pushed with dilute fish emulsion applied each week. By midsummer, lantanas, cape plumbago, heliotrope, various begonias, and assorted geraniums, fuchsias, and all the rest are bushel-basket size, and blooming from top to bottom. When the weather gets hot and bloom is profuse, I increase watering but slow down on feeding, as in our hot climate plants burn out easily. But friends in cooler places tell me that they feed right along, achieving marvelous results. Again it is a matter of adapting technique to situation.

Every hanging plant on the terrace or in the garden needs pinching and grooming from time to time. After all, these specialty plants attract a lot of attention, so they must look their best. Remove spent blossoms at least once a week. At the same time, nip back a shoot here and there to keep plants symmetrical and fairly dense. This is almost automatic; as you walk up, sprinkling can in hand, you water and stare at the plant. You set down the can and pinch here, pick off spent flowers there. It is all part of the daily visit. Just don't get in the habit of neglecting to do it.

A word about watering. Probably you will use tap water and get away with it. Cistern or well water is better if available, and it helps if the can is filled the day before so the water is tempered. Water in the morning so the plants do not dry out through the peak period of water consumption about midday. If you plan to apply liquid fertilizer, give each plant a minidrink of plain water to moisten the soil, then water with the fertilizer solution. Don't fertilize dry soil.

Insect pests and diseases may visit your baskets, boxes, and urns. Pick off the occasional caterpillar. If decay appears, ease up somewhat on water and omit fertilizer for a couple of weeks; cut out decayed stems and pick off bad leaves. A little more sunlight usually helps, too. The real problem will be either white fly or red-spider, or both. There is no point doing anything until they appear, but when they show up, spray weekly with malathion, taking care to coat the undersides of all the leaves. If red-spider alone is the problem, Kelthane is a specific control. Several aerosol garden spray preparations are available, and these are handy for small jobs.

THE MOST SUITABLE ENVIRONMENT

In mild climates near the sea you can use hanging baskets, porch boxes, window boxes, garden urns with pendent plants—all the lovely living arrangements—anywhere in the garden they seem to be appropriate. In the Middle West we are more cautious. Baskets go in the ell of the house or in the sheltered courtyard. Boxes and urns usually are reserved for cloistered entryways and house fronts where an opposing block of buildings affords shelter. Why the difference? Wind. Wind is the nemesis of the gardener; all plants suffer from wind, but baskets with their easily dessicated structure, and boxes and urns, where lots of plants have their roots in a minimum of space, suffer most. Where mild, moisture-laden breezes bathe the foliage, every garden should be freely ornamented with overhead plants. Where hot, dry winds blow, some ingenuity is required. The challenge makes success all the more rewarding.

Well-planted baskets deserve feature spots; use one at the entryway; bracket an oriel window with a pair of them; where the paved terrace stretches the length of the house, space them along the eaves. Baskets are for close viewing; be sure to place them where they are encountered at more or less eye level. If you live in a contemporary home and your garden is partially sheltered by one of those handsome wood grids raised on high posts, a few baskets add elegance. Don't be afraid to experiment in these unusual settings; wire three baskets, one above the other, spacing them at least 2 feet apart. Plant yellow nasturtiums in the top one, orange ones in the middle, and red in the bottom basket. Your column of color will be a knockout.

Baskets look good in Southern gardens hanging from the great horizontal limbs of live oaks and from the lacy ironwork of a gentler era. Rustic baskets planted with ferns, ivies, and foliage plants are also well suited to the shady verandas of log cabins in the North woods. In the inner city, where garden space is at a minimum, an inexpensive series of high metal arches with baskets hanging from the center of each stretches the planting area and screens out the neighbor's back porch. Every garden has a place for a hanging basket or two; on the apartment dweller's balcony, the basket *is* the garden.

Window boxes are used much like baskets, but their location is fixed; they go on the window ledge or on brackets just below the outer sill. These started in Europe, where over 90 percent of city dwellers live in multiple housing with never a chance to garden. The window boxes are their gardens. And how beautiful they look against the stained faces of century-old buildings. The great period for window boxes in America was from 1900 into the Great Depression. Tudor-style houses had them at every window. Cottage-type homes featured huge boxes on heavy brackets under the front windows. Deep porches were the vogue, and window boxes moved from the dark window sill to the balustrade, and became porch boxes.

Today these are in style again. Window boxes offer the renter of a room, the apartment dweller—even the home owner—a chance to have flowers right at hand. We use special soil in the window and porch boxes so our plants do best of any in the neighborhood. At my parents' home, with acres of lawn and extensive flower beds, window boxes are essential to the appearance of the house, and the inhabitants can sit in ease on the porch, watching the hummingbirds feed at lantanas, verbenas, petunias, geraniums, cape plumbago, and other gay blossoms. The annuals are replaced with sprays of berried juniper for winter, and on cold days bluebirds cuddle in the boxes, enjoying the reflected warmth and feasting on berries.

Window boxes go wherever a window calls for them; porch

boxes, too, are situated to meet the needs of architecture and convenience. This may mean that a box is in a windy spot. Then it must be somewhat oversized and the soil fill adapted to retain water without going soggy.

Urns are fairly formidable for most American gardens. Urns call for a cut-stone terrace, marble balustrade, and a head gardener to superintend design and maintenance. There truly is no such thing as a contemporary urn. Urns, in my opinion, cease to be urns unless they are cut stone, lead, or, in Southern gardens, iron. And they demand a formal setting. The proper place for an urn is on a pedestal in the formal garden. With that settled, remember to use plants that match the elegance of their container, and that bear out the formal attitude of the setting.

WINDOW AND PORCH BOX CONSTRUCTION

Boxes are utensils to hold a beautiful array of plants; keep your boxes simple and unadorned. Make them of heavy wood—1-inch planed stock is best. Fit the end pieces and bottom in with long brass screws or zinc-coated nails, both of which resist corrosion, and, if the box is more than 3 feet long, insert tie-pieces every 2 feet along its length, securing these with long screws. Minimum dimensions for any box should be 6 inches clear depth inside, and 6 inches clear width from front to back.

Drainage is essential for good results; drill ½-inch holes every 6 inches in a staggered pattern in the bottom of the box. Porch boxes that rest on a balustrade should have shallow cleats every 2 feet so the bottom is held clear from its support.

Window boxes look best when they are mounted just below the sill of the window. Generally they are as long as the window is wide; if the window is shuttered, and the shutters are no longer than the window pane, extend the box to the outside of both shutters. But if the shutters extend below the window pane, the box must terminate inside the shutters.

Porch boxes may be of any convenient length; three-to-four-foot units look well and are easy to manipulate. Very long boxes fre-

All of the lamiums, including the hardy garden varieties, make interesting basket plants. One of the showiest is *Lamium galeobdolon* var. *variegatum,* with its rich green leaves strongly patterned with bright silver. This one has yellow flowers.

An indoor flower-show arrangement suitable for displaying hanging plants in the garden. The multiple-armed stand supports baskets and boxes of home-grown azalea, ivy geranium, rosemary, Swedish-ivy, and fuchsia. Displays of this sort are featured each year at the Philadelphia Flower Show.

The zebra-plant as a specimen for a garden basket. *Zebrina pendula* leaves develop intensified coloration—deeper purple, brighter silver-green stripes—in daylight; but direct sunlight all day may scald the upper leaves. Dappled shade is best for this plant and its relatives.

Living sculpture may be used as a hanging ornament in your garden. Make a frame of the desired shape of fairly stiff iron rods and wrap with hardware cloth or chicken wire. Moss as for a basket, and fill with a porous soil mixture (large forms may be designed to be hollow). Dibble small plants, in this case, English ivy, over the surface of the form, and train the shoots by pegging them down with U-shaped pieces of wire.

quently bulge due to pressure from soil, water, and expanding roots.

Empty the outside boxes after frost discolors the plants in the fall. Hose them clean, and when they are quite dry, repaint the inside with a neutral preservative such as Cuprinol. Boxes may afterward be filled with sawdust or other light, inert material to hold evergreen boughs arranged as if they were growing; then the house looks dressed in winter.

In the old days urns were filled with layers of drainage material and topped off with potting compost. There were always two or three men around to help lift and empty the thing. Today, with modern plastics available, I suggest using a liner. It makes work easier and protects a valuable urn. Your neighborhood nurseryman can supply you with a semi-flexible plastic container used for small trees and shrubs that will fit in your urn. Trim the top down with a tin snips if it is too high. Be sure that liner and urn have drain holes.

Box, basket, or urn, we have to be concerned with drainage. A typical wire, wood, or plastic basket is no problem. But a box or urn requires special handling. Cover the holes in the bottom with curved pieces of broken flower pot so pebbles cannot choke them. Then pour in, carefully so as not to displace the crocks, an inch or two of coarse gravel, granite chips, or broken crocks. Over this goes a similar layer of smaller gravel, and finally a layer of coarse peat screenings. The drainage bed needs to be a minimum of 3 inches thick—more is better. If your water is hard, mix hardwood charcoal chips freely through the drainage bed to absorb excess minerals.

The lilac-colored lantana with drooping branches and small leaves is *L. montevidensis*, sold by plantsmen as *L. sellowiana*. Ideal for urns, boxes, or baskets, a rooted cutting in a 3-inch pot may develop into a bushel-basket-sized specimen through the summer months. Ample water and frequent applications of fertilizer are the way to do it.

5

Outdoors in Box, Urn, and Basket

Landscape design seldom calls for window boxes, urns on the garden wall, large pots of flowers on the terrace, or hanging baskets in the arbor. These are the personal touches that give a garden individual charm. The enthusiast who specializes in fuchsias or tuberous begonias must grow basket plants to make his collection complete. Often a collection of house plants, including those in hanging baskets and pots, comes to the dappled shade of the garden for summer. And these usually make first-rate garden decorations. But there are other possibilities.

Many familiar annuals used for bedding make perfectly good plants for container growing. Though they have a more-or-less upright habit in the bed, they may droop gracefully when planted in a box, basket, or urn, revealing a charm you never suspected. Some of the annual flowering vines may be so trained. Then there are plants most suitable for strawberry jars. And everyone should use hanging baskets of flowering plants where people sit in the garden. To lounge in a comfortable chair on the terrace in the dappled shade of a grand old tree is pure pleasure; if bright flowers peep from baskets hung from the branches of that tree, it is even nicer. Most outdoor plants suitable for basket growing are familiar; they need no description, just suggestions for use.

ANNUALS
FOR HANGING BASKETS, BOXES, AND URNS

In Full Sun

Sweet Alyssum, *Lobularia maritima* cultivars; 2–4 inches high, spreading to 12 inches, white, pink, purple; decumbent to trailing.

Browallia, *B. speciosa major* and cultivars; 10–15-inch plant, blue, white; bushy.

Cape-marigold, *Dimorphotheca auranticus* cultivars; 8–12 inches high, yellow, white; sprawling.

Coleus, cultivars; 10–24 inches high, multicolored foliage; bushy to decumbent.

Cup-flower, *Nierembergia* species and cultivars; 6 inches high, spreading to 12 inches, blue-violet, white; decumbent.

Floss-flower, *Ageratum houstonianum* cultivars; 6–10 inches high, blue shades; bushy.

Lobelia, *L. erinus* cultivars; 5 inches high, spreading 10–15 inches, blue shades, white, magenta-pink; decumbent to trailing.

Monkey-flower, *Mimulus X tigrinus* cultivars; 10 inches high, yellow, orange, red, rust; decumbent to bushy.

Bush morning-glory, *Convolvulus mauritanicus* cultivars; deep blue, white, or white and yellow throat; bushy.

Nasturtium, *N. tropaeolum majus* cultivars; 6–8 inches high, spreading 8–24 inches; cream, yellow, orange, rose, red; bushy-decumbent to trailing.

Nemesia, *N. strumosa* dwarf cultivars; 8–12 inches high, most colors, bushy to sprawling. Cool climates only.

Phacelia, *P. campanularia,* 6 inches high, blue, decumbent.

Phlox, *P. drummondi* dwarf cultivars; 5–10 inches, white, buff, salmon, pink, red; bushy.

Garden pinks, *Dianthus latifolius* and *D. plumarius* cultivars; 6–12 inches high; white, pink, rose; sprawling to decumbent.

Rose-moss, *Portulaca grandiflora* cultivars; 3 inches high, spreading to 10 inches; white, yellow, orange, pink, cerise; decumbent.

Above left, trailing kinds of lobelia grow in a very decumbent manner; the bedding lobelias, as in this basket of 'Blue Stone', make more upright growth, but the outer stems will spread downward to a degree. Both are fine container plants in the summer garden.

Above right, Browallia cultivars bloom all summer; flowers may be medium blue, light blue, or white. Upright forms are suitable in the center of baskets or urns; these also are valuable in window boxes and in terrace pots. Browallias bloom best in full sun but also make quite a nice showing in bright shade.

Below: Bush-form sweet peas make delightful flower-covered little plants for boxes, baskets, and pots in the garden. The strain shown here, growing in a wood box of contemporary design, is Bijou. For best results, start these in pots and move several plants into the display container when they are about 6 inches high.

Snapdragon, *Antirrhinum* dwarf cultivars; 6–8 inches; all colors except blue shades; bushy.

Verbena, *V. X hortensis* cultivars; 4–8 inches, spreading 12–24 inches; white, pink, red, purple. Sprawling to almost trailing.

In Shade

Many annuals for sun will bloom to a degree in part shade.

Begonia, *B. semperflorens gracilis* cultivars; 8–12 inches high; white, pink, red flowers; foliage green or bronze-red; bushy. Some strains also excellent for full sun.

Sultana, *Impatiens* cultivars; 6–12 inches high; orange, pink, rose, red, white; foliage green or bronze-red; select the dwarf, spreading sorts; sprawling.

Periwinkle, *Vinca rosea* cultivars; white, rose (with eye-spot) ; 6 inches high, spreading to 15 inches; decumbent; select the dwarf, spreading kinds.

Wishbone-flower, *Torenia fournieri;* blue, purple markings, 12 inches high, bushy.

OLD STANDBYS FOR BOXES, URNS, AND BASKETS

These plants have stood the test of time; they, or more likely, their forerunners, were used for container gardening way back when. They are still good, and many are better today due to continuous upgrading through breeding and selection. If you make these the backbone of your container garden, you will not go wrong.

Cape Plumbago, *Plumbago larpentae;* see Chapter 6.

Geranium, *Pelargonium* species and cultivars; 12–18 inches high; white, pink, salmon, rose, and red; bushy or decumbent. Choose the modern strains grown from seed for virus-free, vigorous plants (as the Carefree strain) . Ivy geranium cultivars, *P. peltatum,* make ideal plants for foreground planting in hanging containers.

Where summer weather is not too hot, tuberous begonias are among the showiest and best-loved basket plants for the garden. This photo shows a special container made by hollowing out a large piece of osmunda fiber. Quite porous, it allows aeration for healthy roots and good drainage.

Left, the black-eyed-Susan vines make excellent basket plants for the summer garden. These are equally good in urns, as the normally ascending vines bloom freely when grown as trailers. Colors are cream, yellow, orange, and tangerine shades, often with a dark eye.

Right, Achimenes produce a profusion of stems with flowers from top to bottom when grown in containers in the summer garden. Ideal for terrace pots, these may be used in window boxes and porch boxes, too. Contrary to the accepted idea, they grow vigorously and bloom freely in full sun as long as the soil is kept moist.

Fuchsia, see Chapter 6.

Heliotrope, see Chapter 6.

Lantana, see Chapter 6.

Petunia, *Petunia* cultivars; 8–15 inches; white, pink, rose, red, scarlet, bicolor; bushy to trailing. All petunias "hang" well, but select flower style to accent your design—small or large, plain or ruffled, single or double. Watch for the special Swiss pendent strains in seed catalogues.

Shrimp-plant, *Beloperone guttata* and B. 'Yellow Queen'; 15–18 inches high; orange-rusty red or yellow; bushy; fine urn centerpiece.

Two forms of the fuchsia blossom: right, the graceful streamlined beauty of the single fuchsia 'Cardinal'; 'Swingtime', with "ballet-girl" flowers, typifies the double fuchsia blossom.

FOR VERY EARLY BLOOM
WITH TRAILING PLANTS

Probably these plants will have to be replaced for summer color, but how nice to have the garden especially dressed for spring! Combine with spring bulbs.

Candytuft, *Iberis umbellata,* dwarf cultivars; 10–15 inches high; white, pink, violet, purple; upright to decumbent.

English Daisy, *Bellis perennis* cultivars; 5–10 inches high; white, pink, rose, red; upright, from leafy rosette.

Forget-me-not, *Myosotis* species and cultivars; 4–10 inches high; blue, pink; bushy to decumbent.

Pansy, *Viola tricolor* cultivars; 6–10 inches high; most colors; bushy-decumbent.

Viola, *V. tricolor* and *V. cornuta* cultivars; 5–10 inches high; most colors, sprawling to decumbent.

Wallflower, *Cheiranthus cheiri* dwarf cultivars; 8–12 inches high; yellow, orange, purple, brown; spreading upright.

ANNUAL VINES FOR BASKETS

A number of the annual flowering vines make good basket subjects. The trick is to use the standard potting compost of equal parts loam, brown peat, and sand (with a little perlite added in hot climates), and pinch young plants to get full branching early, then train runners round and round. One variety to a basket, please!

Black-eyed-Susan-vine, *Thunbergia alata* and *T. gibsonii* and cultivars; cream, yellow, buff, orange, often with purplish eye; full sun to half shade.

Canary-bird-vine, *Tropaeolum peregrinum;* yellow; handsome foliage; full sun; very adaptable.

Cardinal-climber, *Quamoclit sloteri;* white-throated scarlet flowers, mid-green foliage; full sun to half-shade.

Cypress vine, *Quamoclit pennata* (*Ipomaea quamoclit*) ; white or
    scarlet, finely divided ferny foliage; full sun to half-shade. This
    and cardinal-climber are good hummingbird plants.
Morning-glory, *Ipomoea* species and cultivars; see under *Ipomoea* in
    Chapter 3. Refer to 'Japanese Imperial' and 'Imperial Giant
    Fringed' strains.
Nasturtium, *Tropaeolum majus,* climbing cultivars; yellow, orange,
    red; full sun, no wind.
Sweet Pea; *Lathyrus odoratus* cultivars; use only the bush and dwarf
    forms; heat-resistant kinds make best basket plants; white, pink,
    rose, red, purple; full sun. These also are suitable for boxes and
    urns in *cool* climates.

HERBS AS PENDENT PLANTS

Several culinary and fragrant herbs develop into graceful hanging plants when grown in boxes, urns, or baskets. My preference is
not to use them in baskets, but to work them into terrace pots and
urns, and into strawberry jars. All want fast drainage, moderately
rich, coarse soil, and full sun. Allow to dry before rewatering. Kinds
that hang gracefully include the dwarf lavenders and rosemarys,
winter savory, most of the thymes, (including the creeping, garden
sorts) , sweet marjoram, and lady's-mantle (*Alchemilla vulgaris*) .

DECUMBENT PLANTS FOR STRAWBERRY JARS

A few people grow strawberry plants in strawberry jars; most
often hen-and-chickens seem to fill the little pockets. And they look
very well, too. But any number of dangling, tough plants can be used
in the strawberry jar. Just ensure proper drainage and soil conditions. If the jar has no hole in the bottom, knock one in with a star-
chisel and hammer. Pile several inches of sizable pieces of curved,
broken flower pot (crocks) over this and then add the fill soil. I find
that it pays to stand a cardboard mailing tube (both ends removed)
in the center and pour potting soil all round it. Then fill the tube

with coarse sand or granite grit and withdraw it gently so a column of drainage aggregate remains in the center of the jar.

Plants that make up well in the pockets of a strawberry jar include:

Full Sun	Half to Full Shade
portulaca	Kenilworth-ivy
sedums of all sorts	variegated ground-ivy
achimenes	strawberry-begonia (*Saxifraga sarmentosa*)
dusty millers	creeping fig (South)

My idea of a fine ornament near the kitchen door is a strawberry jar with the various herbs listed on page 79 in the pockets, and a 'Patio' tomato planted in the top. One of the prettiest jars I ever saw was quite large, planted entirely with silver-foliaged plants; the dusty millers, senecios, cinerarias and chrysanthemums, and silver santo-linas—charming against the dusty rose of the old Italian jar.

ODDS AND ENDS

My notebook lists a number of plants that spill down or hang over and that do not fit any of the preceding categories. Yet they are too nice to leave out of a book on plants that droop, dangle, or trail. Briefly, they are:

Achimenes: I have mentioned these before in Chapter 3. They deserve more attention. Among the toughest of the gesneriads, they are also, in my experience, the most floriferous. A neighbor has a window box of these. They are started in early spring under plant lights in pots. Then they go into the box and, when growth is active, manure water is their reward. By June they are starting to bloom. By July the face of the box is covered with foliage and flowers. The display gets bigger and better until frost ends it for the year. Her variety is the old-fashioned *A. patens,* with large lilac blossoms. By all means use achimenes at the front of your shady boxes and urns. Plant baskets of them to hang from the trees. Store the scaly tubers in a paper bag over winter and repot in fresh soil next season. You can keep them going over winter in a bright window, but to me achimenes mean warm summer. They bloom in shade; they bloom better in sun. Achimenes grow in the house; they *thrive* in the garden. Mine spend the winter in a paper bag in the cellar.

Hedera: English-ivy cultivars are many and varied. Some belong in the house, others look better in the garden. While ivies thrive in baskets, I think they look wrong in them. For house use, I like them in pots set in ring brackets up and down the sides of a window. In the garden, I feel that the green kinds look best in the ground-cover beds, but some of the variegated ones look nice in wide, shallow pots on the garden wall where the stems trail downward.

Lycopersicum esculentum, L. pimpinellifolium, and cultivars: tomato, in English. The second species listed is a bushy, limp thing, rather small-leaved and bearing beautiful sprays of delicious little tomatoes, pea to cherry size. Grown in a hanging basket, carefully trained to trail down, this makes a beautiful decoration, besides supplying the salad with tomatoes all summer. Several small-stature tomato cultivars have been introduced recently such as 'Patio'; all are nice in jars, boxes (in the kitchen garden) , or in baskets.

Polygonum capitatum: an annual, easy from seed, thrives in full sun. Creeping stems are well furnished with bronze foliage and produce dozens of pink flower heads somewhat like clover. Good in boxes, baskets, urns, and jars as a decumbent edger. Let the children plant a basket of this and care for it.

Punica granatum nanum: dwarf pomegranate is a favorite of mine. I think the shiny leaves and orange blossoms are fresh and beautiful. And when a walnut-sized pomegranate—a *real* pomegranate—shows up, it seems a miracle. Grow this in a small pot and set it on a pedestal made of an oiled and rubbed 4-by-4 piece of wood about a foot high. It is a wonderful centerpiece for the terrace table. Keep the plant going over winter on a sunny windowsill.

6

Tender Woody Plants with Flowers

Once you become a hanging-basket enthusiast, woody perennial trailers will become the backbone of your collection. Unlike annuals, these go on year after year, becoming larger and more spectacular as time passes. If, that is, you have a place to overwinter them.

There are two ways to cope with these; start cuttings for new plants or renew your old plants in spring, enjoy them through a flower-filled summer, and discard them in fall, or else plan to carry them over. None overwinters well in the average home. If you have a cool, bright garden room, a *bright,* cool basement window, or a small greenhouse, fine. Your flowering woody plants will stay with you for years. But don't forgo growing these if you feel you cannot hold them over. First-year plants make a fine show, and you get more than your money's worth. You can let them go with the first frost and replace them next season.

PENDENT FUCHSIAS

Fuchsias, those marvelous Edwardian shrubs from the always cool, mist-washed mild tip of South America, grow upright, or sprawl, or make pendulous branches. Avoid the upright types, skip

Fuchsia 'Swingtime' greets visitors at the front entrance; hung at the eave edge where the plant gets only morning and late afternoon sunlight and enjoys shelter from the wind, this fine plant is in full flower through the entire summer. Over winter it is cut back and hung in a cool, bright basement window where it is kept in a semi-dormant condition.

the sprawlers, unless one has a blossom that you simply cannot withstand, and concentrate on the drooping kinds. Fuchsia breeders have been very busy, so you have your choice of double flowers or single; large, highly developed flowers or modest, tubular ones that resemble their wild ancestors; foliage that is rich olive-green (always with a hint of ruby on leaf stems and tender stalks), or, rarely, variegated. It pays to deal with a specialist when buying fuchsias, as his great list of cultivars is sure to offer just the plant you want.

Young fuchsia plants usually arrive as tender, recently rooted cuttings 3 to 4 inches high, and just out of a 2-inch pot. Given proper care, they will grow fast; choose your basket accordingly. I prefer to pot up newly arrived plants in fuchsia compost and grow them on for a month or 6 weeks; as soon as they are established, I begin pinching.

When a new shoot has made 3 or 4 pairs of leaves, I pinch it to 1 or 2 pairs.

To plant a fuchsia in a basket, moss the container with an extra-thick mat of presoaked and squeezed moss. Fuchsia compost is 2 parts soil from your best flower bed, 1 part garden compost, leafmold, or well-decayed cow manure (if you are a fuchsia enthusiast you *cannot* get along without cow manure) , and ½ part clean sand. To ½ bushel of this add a cup of fish-meal fertilizer. You will learn quickly that, for some reason, fuchsias respond poorly to most chemical fertilizers, but dote on various organics, especially fish-emulsion solution. Many expert fuchsia growers use this exclusively.

Set your young plant in the center of the container—I recommend a 12-inch-wide, deep wire basket, mossed, and with a shallow fill of fuchsia compost. Adjust the height of the plant so the level of the soil ball is about an inch below the top of the basket, and plant rather firmly. Stake it until it becomes established, and set in a bright, sunless, windless place for 3 or 4 days. Mist the foliage daily or more often, and water daily. Begin feeding when growth resumes, and feed weekly so long as the plant is in flower. I use commercial fish emulsion, but dilute it a third more than the recommended dosage.

Fuchsias want to grow in full, bright shade though in cool climates they will tolerate a little early-morning or late-afternoon sun. They do not do well when subjected to air currents, and persistent wind soon kills them. The potting soil must never dry.

Pinch back overly vigorous shoots that break out now and again from older wood. Also pinch an occasional side shoot; you may sacrifice a few buds, but a well-grown plant quickly replaces them, and you will be shaping your specimen. As the fuchsia is a major showpiece, I feel that it is best grown alone in the basket. But I once saw a fine one with close-clipped baby's-tears grown over the bottom of the basket to hide the moss, and it was quite handsome.

To save fuchsia plants, stop fertilizer 6 weeks before frost date in the fall. Three weeks later, slow down on watering—never allow the plants to dry completely—to discourage new growth (and flower buds) . As outdoor-grown fuchsias are almost sure to be infested with white fly and possibly a few aphids, spray twice a week for 6 or 8 treatments. Move indoors, to a 40° to 45° F. room, if possible, and grow in fairly dry air, watering only rarely to preserve some foliage. In February or March, repot if necessary (some experts recommend delaying repotting until growth has resumed), prune heavily, and begin to water *moderately*—no fertilizer.

Pruning is critical; butchery seems to get the best results. I save the main trunk, the branches that break from it, and about 2 inches of the branches that break from these. With plants more than 3 years old, cut back only 1-year-old wood and a little of the 2-year-old.

A month before frostfree date, move your fuchsias to a warmer place, 45° to 55° F., and increase daily water. As new growth becomes general, begin feeding, first biweekly, then weekly, then twice weekly.

Fuchsias are easy from cuttings. Stick 5- or 6-inch cuttings singly in small pots of sandy soil, in midwinter, at a 70° F. window and covered with a thin plastic bag, in summer on a shady, windless porch. You may use hormones, special rooting media, and other paraphernalia, but this is not necessary as long as you use vigorous shoots, healthy soil, and clean pots.

A list of cultivars would be pointless; look at the catalogue of a specialist or visit a local source and pick those that look prettiest to you. I prefer not to be without at least one 'Swingtime'; the species *F. procumbens,* with its odd yellow-and-blue flowers and plentiful magenta-crimson berries, is fun, but difficult to find.

LANTANAS

Lantanas are a favorite of mine. They outgrow the weeds in my hot, windy Middle West garden, they require very little, and they adapt to numerous situations. Using a fuchsia in a mixed planting would be like sticking an orchid in a mixed garden bouquet. But lantanas hodgepodge together with other plants in window boxes, mixed baskets, and urns, and look just great.

One species of lantana is trailing; *L. montevidensis,* usually sold in the American trade as *L. sellowiana.* This species has long, sprawling, rather finely divided branches, harsh, quite small leaves, and a myriad of lavender flower heads. This is one I do like to grow singly in an urn or basket, as it makes a great cool lavender fountain long before midsummer. But it, too, mixes well with other plants in boxes, baskets, and urns.

Lantanas have been a favorite with hybridizers in recent years. As crops of volunteer seedlings spring up freely under mature plants, I suspect that most of the new forms and color blends are selections from a chance breeding, but nonetheless the new ones are good. Most are chosen for purity or brilliance of color, floriferous habit, and in some cases, growth habit. Most dealers offer two groups; those that grow into bush form, more-or-less upright, and those that the trade calls ground-cover kinds. These low ones are ideal for container growing as they quickly become pendent. But even the bush sorts may be pruned to downward growth.

We used to think of lantanas as plants with flower heads of burnt orange and yellow, or pinkish lavender and pale yellow. Today plants come with one-color flower clusters of white, cream, several shades of yellow, orange, lilac, lavender, and even a kind of magenta red. There are bicolors (usually the inner flowers are some shade of yellow) and tricolors. There is one with florets of various colors in one head. These exciting new cultivars are coming largely from southern California. Monrovia Nursery Company is responsible for a great listing of them (wholesale only), and your local garden-shop specialist can order in a fine selection for the neighborhood.

The best site for lantanas is full sun (however, they flower freely with just half-day sunlight) and wind protection if possible, though they withstand some wind if kept well watered. The soil mixture is 2 parts rich garden soil and 1 part damp peat, compost, or leafmold. If your loam is heavy, add sand. If your soil is more than slightly acid, add a few chunks of charcoal to the mix. I find that plants grown in a windy exposure wilt less if as much as a fourth (by volume) of *coarse* perlite is added to the mixture.

Too generous feeding of lantanas produces lush foliage and few flowers. These plants do well on all common liquid house-plant fertilizers; feed singly grown plants *half strength* solution twice monthly. In mixed plantings, do not fertilize near the lantanas, just give them extra water. Their long roots will go after the nutrients.

When in vigorous growth, lantanas need water frequently; never let the soil dry. Six weeks prior to frost date in the fall, stop all feeding and begin withholding water to harden off the plants. As the leaves toughen, you can let the soil dry completely on top before watering, and the leaves will not wilt. Move the plants to full, bright shade (outdoors) to accustom them to reduced light, and spray for white fly and aphids as for fuchsias. Move into a chilly room, a bright, cold basement window, or cold greenhouse. The easiest way with these is to clip back tender growth and water sparingly at 10-day to 2-week intervals. In the cold greenhouse they go under the bench (away from heat pipes) to keep them dormant and out of the way.

In February or March handle as fuchsias; prune back, repot, or replant as needed when growth buds appear, and gradually increase water and warmth. It is easy to keep a lantana for a hundred years or so, and huge weeping and standard forms are worth it. But I prefer to start fresh yearly with little fellows in window boxes and urns.

When early daffodils bloom, take lantana cuttings; select firm green shoots and cut with a razor blade just below a pair of leaves. Remove these leaves, dip the cut end in rooting hormone and stick in a sand-peat or perlite-peat mixture, preferably in a place with gentle bottom heat. Cover with a loose plastic sheet and keep at 65° to 75° F. These root quickly and should be potted up while roots are short. For overwintering young plants, take cuttings in August. Grow these young plants, fed and watered, in a sunny, cool window or greenhouse. Overwinter to supply more cuttings for spring. White fly will be a constant problem, so be prepared to spray. House plant aerosol insecticides are convenient for indoor bug control.

Lantana species, save for *L. montevidensis,* are little grown and rarely available. Look for the new, brightly colored patented or trade-mark-protected sorts.

CAPE PLUMBAGO

Clear, light-blue flowers are hard to come by, but here is a good blue-flowered plant and one easy to grow. Stuck with the common name of leadwort, and properly called *Plumbago capensis,* growers usually call it Cape plumbago. This is a truly woody shrub; in the tropics it reaches 10 to 15 feet. In an urn or window box it is easily kept to 18 inches, and when upright shoots are cut back continuously, soon it spills out and down. There is also a white-flowered form.

The compost for this plant is equal parts coarse brown peat and leafmold, and 1/2 part each loam and sand. If you carry plants over winter, grow them at chilly room temperature, keep rather dry until March, then move them to a warm window, increase water, and when new growth begins to show, prune rather harshly. Plumbago mixes well with window-box plants, makes a fine show alone or with other plants in an urn, and, if carefully pruned, makes a spectacular basket plant. While blooming, it should get half-strength fertilizer twice a week; the soil should never dry out.

Unenthusiastic about intense sunlight combined with reflected heat and light from a white building, Cape plumbago will take almost any exposure as long as it is supplied with ample water and nutrients. When a shoot blooms out, cut it back to one or two leaves to force new, flower-bearing growths.

Side shoots with a heel, dipped in rooting hormone and stuck into a mixture of equal parts peat and perlite, root readily from March through August. These quickly become flowering size.

A special way with Cape plumbago is cascade-training. Use the same system, as fully explained for chrysanthemums in Chapter 7, but this is easier. Start a plant in an 8-inch pot and stake up a vertical shoot; pinch this at 6 to 8 inches. Pinch the branches, too, and stake these upright, fanned out flat. Gradually bend the main support near the ground line and, as the plant grows, continue to fan it outward, gradually bending it down. As the main stem becomes quite brittle, bending must be very gradual.

HELIOTROPE

Not a naturally pendent plant by any means, heliotrope, *Heliotropium arborescens,* can be encouraged to make pendent growth by pinching hard while young to get long laterals which, when heavy with flowers, droop down from an urn or box. My favorite use for these is in a porch box where the delicious scent is close to people. The heads of purple flowers are impressive in a formal urn.

Easy to grow from seed, you will get a population of plants only a few of which will be strongly scented. Better visit the local greenhouse and sniff each plant, selecting the highly scented ones. Heliotrope is a true tropical from Peru and thrives in a warm, sunny place. The best compost is equal parts good garden loam, leafmold, and sand. Keep well watered always, and feed biweekly while in blossom. Liquid manure or fish emulsion solution gives the finest flowers and foliage, but synthetic fertilizers are adequate.

To carry over your favorite heliotrope, reduce watering outdoors to harden it, and gradually move it to reduced light. Then bring it inside to a bright sunny window in a cool room. You will get some winter flowering and, unless you sprayed regularly, lots of white fly.

FLOWERING-MAPLE

Most of these shrubby hollyhock relatives are not suited for hanging containers or for pendulous growth. But the semivining *Abutilon megapotamicum* makes a wonderful basket or box plant. Grow it where you will encounter the unusual furled yellow-and-scarlet blossoms nose to nose.

Sow seeds a ¼-inch deep or take cuttings in March. Grow young plants in pots, pinching occasionally to get several stems. The potting compost is 2 parts garden loam and 1 part each peat and sand. Any general box or urn mixture is adequate. These want a warm place, full sun, and ample water. Three young plants in a 12-inch basket can be trained into a real showpiece by midsummer. Or use them as pendent decoration in a window box or urn. Pinch back shoots that want to grow upward.

When pot-grown this flowering-maple is a good house plant for winter. Average room temperature, a place near a window, and ample water are all that is required. Flowering-maple requires little or no fertilizer.

LOTUS

I have always suspected that several members of the lotus family would make good basket plants, and have had handsome, trouble-free baskets with the common bird's-foot trefoil, *L. corniculatus.* I hope you will try it, too. But the really showy basket species is *L. berthelotii,* from the Canary Islands.

This species, with no common name, makes a silver cloud of finely divided foliage on much branched wiry stems. Filled with well-grown plants, your basket will be hidden by midsummer. A florist friend gave me my first start of this, and I thought it was just for foliage. Then, one day one side of the box—it was growing in a wood basket made of redwood 1-by-1's—was starred with great parrot's-beak-style blossoms, scarlet, lightly streaked with chocolate. Since then, I have seen the plant in beautiful condition in several Montana parks, in Arizona, and in California. It is available as small plants from mail-order companies.

The correct compost is 2 parts sandy loam, 1 part leafmold and ½ part each finely broken hardwood charcoal and river sand. For the greenhouse or plant room, grow it near the ventilator, just under the glass. In the garden, give it a sunny, windfree location. Afternoon shade is tolerated. Grow this on the dry side; water it moderately in the spring when it is making its greatest growth, then cut down during the summer. Very weak fertilizer once a month, spring through late summer, is sufficient.

In my estimation, *L. berthelotii* should be kept for basket culture. But I have seen it used effectively in porch and window boxes and in urns. Also, it makes a fine pendent edging for raised planter beds. Well-grown plants droop naturally about 2 feet. The upright growth is negligible.

OTHER LEGUMES

Two other legumes, related to *Lotus,* are *Swainsona galegifolia* var. *coronillaefolia* and *Clianthus puniceus.* The first sometimes is called violet Darling river-pea, and the latter usually is known as parrot's-bill clianthus. These shrubby legumes from Australia make fine basket specimens when young. Pot them in 2 parts garden loam and 1 part each damp brown peat and sand, with some broken brick and charcoal mixed through the compost. Sensitive to chilly weather and killed by frost, these want a sunny spot out of wind.

Swainsona will have to be pruned to make it droop well; cut out upright stems and encourage limp side shoots. The vining clianthus will dangle of its own accord. Grow both on the dry side, and water only in early morning. Give them very dilute organic fertilizer once a month while they are making new leafy growth. Difficult to carry over in the house, these are no trouble in the plant room or greenhouse when grown in a cool, airy place near the glass. Both are difficult to locate—generally you have to talk the horticulturist at a botanic garden out of a cutting. Presently I am on the track of other clianthus species that a friend tells me make fine container plants Down Under.

Petunias used two ways. Above, hanging baskets of petunias compliment those in the terrace containers and in the foundation bed. Left, a wood structure supports boxes of petunias at the top, with baskets of the same cultivar below. In both photos the container petunias are various colors of Cascade strain.

7

Petunias, Begonias, and Chrysanthemums

PETUNIAS

If I had to choose just one kind of plant to grow in my window boxes, hanging baskets, and terrace pots—a plant for indoors as well as the garden—it would be petunias. Technically, the petunia is a perennial, but because it is killed by heavy frost, we usually grow it as an annual. As petunias thrive in almost any kind of garden soil, as long as the drainage is good, there is no point in spending time on technicalities of composts. But you must remember to fertilize your petunias lightly every week or two once they begin to flower, and if you are faithful about pinching out spent blossoms to prevent formation of seed pods, you will keep your plants in flower until frost bites, or until you discard them.

To learn the horticultural classification of petunias is to gain considerable insight into how different strains can be used in the garden. All too often we overlook the breeding behind our garden plants, and it shows in our misuse of the various breeding lines. As some petunias have been bred for forcing, others for box and urn planting, still others for baskets, and yet another group for bedding, no wonder the amateur gets confused. Never mind; any petunia planted in a raised container will sprawl, then drape downward while blooming profusely. But for best effect, use the various strains the right way.

Our garden petunias seem to have originated from crosses between two wild South American species. They have come a long way. The simplified classification presented here is assembled from retail seed catalogues; you should be able to find examples of all these strains in the catalogue of a first-rate company.

P. hybrida grandiflora. To 1 foot in height, spreading somewhat more than a foot; these have simple, tailored blossoms, unruffled. Often they are sweet-scented. This is primarily a bedding strain, but good for small containers. 'Rosy Morn', 'Sugarplum', and 'Bright Star' are cultivars in this group.

P. hybrida grandiflora superbissima. To 1 foot in height, but usually with somewhat decumbent stems; these bear 5- to 7-inch ruffled single blossoms, usually with beautiful veining patterns in the throat. Somewhat susceptible to damage from wind and rain, but superb for all sorts of containers. Examples include 'Giants of California' and 'Prince of Wurtemburg.'

P. hybrida grandiflora flore plena. These are the double forms of the grandifloras, usually; as some breeders have concentrated on flower form only, the plants may be leggy and, in a given batch, remarkably varied. Still, the double petunias get better every year, and it would be difficult to imagine boxes and urns without them. Most modern doubles fall into this group.

P. hybrida pendula. These are the balcony petunias. They have been selected for their decumbent form, close branching and free flowering. With upright growth usually limited to a stem or two reaching to 1 foot, most branches grow downward, extending as much as 2 feet. I think these look best in window and porch boxes; they are out of proportion for all but the largest urns, and if used in terrace pots, before the season is half over they are down to and sprawling on the pavement. Watch for the Swiss strains sold as "Bernese Basket Petunias." These come in red and white (the colors of Switzerland) and make an especially fine show. But our American balcony petunias need no apology. They belong in every window box.

P. nana compacta. These are the newest bedding petunias, re-developed from an older strain. With a cloud of modest-sized flowers in brilliant colors, they make little mounded plants of great charm, but of limited value for container-growing.

Which petunias do I select for my window boxes? The Cascade series, white, coral, clear pinks and near-red thrive for me, are heavily scented, and the hawk moths come to the windows at night to feed from them; they are my main crop. For the terrace pots Giants of California make the best show, and I particularly favor the New Horizon strain with its melting colors of old rose, Dresden pink, strawberry, copper-rose and lilac-pink. Each window box at our farm gets its share of the bedding sorts: 'Apple-blossom', the Satin series, the Joy mixture, and every petunia in the catalogue described as "velvety purple," because to me *nothing* is more beautiful than a rich, royal-purple petunia.

So much for petunias in the garden. I trust you are inspired to plant a few baskets, boxes, and urns of them for next summer. Do you know about petunias as house plants? They require a cool room with a full flood of light. A well-pinched plant in a 5-inch pot set on a glass shelf makes as good a flowering house plant as I know. With periodic feeding it will bloom all winter. You can pinch to keep it bushy or you can let long shoots develop that hang way down, with flowers strung here and there along their length. Here is a place where those huge, ruffled ones really make a show, as no wind or water ever spoils the blossoms. Grow a batch of these for the garden; pick out the ones with the prettiest flowers, then cull them, marking just the best-scented ones. In August root 4- to 6-inch cuttings in barely damp sand—I use a sterile pot and cover it with a plastic dome—to be potted up in September. Or dig a garden plant and pot it up; cut it back to half its spread and grow it on in the garden for a week or two, as it will establish more quickly. Then move it indoors.

TUBEROUS BEGONIAS IN BASKETS

If ever a plant was bred for container growing, the pendent tuberous begonia fits the bill. You just cannot imagine this plant bedded out in the garden, with its dangling flowers, face downward, in the mud. Tuberous begonias grow best in cool, misty places. I have trouble with them in my prairie garden as they dislike the heat and go to pieces in the wind. Still, I can grow a few in the lee of the house, on the north side, and they are worth the trouble.

Buy modest-sized tubers of these; the expensive, saucer-sized ones make very little more show and sometimes are old and tired, so that they produce lots of leaves and few flowers. Almost fill a shallow garden flat (drain holes are essential) with a starting medium; specialists favor sieved homemade leafmold, pasteurized by pouring quantities of boiling water through it. Or rub brown peat through a $\frac{1}{4}$-inch sieve and dampen it. Press your tubers down into the medium, 6 inches apart, and cover with *loose,* damp medium. Best results come with already sprouted tubers; to bring sprouts out before starting, lay them in a warm, humid place for a few days.

Roots will break out from the bottom and sides of the tubers in about seven days. Keep the medium barely moist. Overwatering brings decay. The flat should be in filtered sunlight or given 8 to 10 hours of fluorescent light, a foot below the bulbs at first, and kept at a temperature of about 65° F. When the plants have made about 5 inches of growth and are heavily rooted, pot up singly in 8-inch pots.

Place a generous layer of broken crock in the bottom of the pot. Fill with potting mix. An easy compost requires 4 parts well-decayed leafmold—homemade or commercial—1 part each garden loam and clean sand. Some specialists favor substituting well-rotted cow manure for half the leafmold. Into the soil for an 8-inch pot mix 2 tablespoons fish meal. Adjust the plant so it is set slightly deeper than it grew in the rooting flat, with the finished level of the soil $\frac{1}{2}$ inch below the rim of the pot. Water thoroughly, then not again until the surface shows signs of dryness. Keep the plants in subdued light, free of wind, for a few days; then move them into brighter light.

Upright-growing tuberous begonias are valuable for boxes, urns, terrace tubs, and even in baskets when a mixed planting is used. A plant such as the one shown, sturdy, just coming into blossom, makes a beautiful centerpiece for a small container "garden" when combined with various trailing plants, such as lobelia and small ferns.

While upright tuberous begonias are rigorously pinched and trained, I prefer to leave pendulous sorts alone while young unless they fail to branch, in which case I pinch once or twice. At potting time, I pinch out the tips of all shoots. When the plants have made a good ball of roots in the pot—4 to 8 weeks—move them on to a basket.

You may grow basket varieties in a heavily mossed basket, using the above potting compost, or you may choose another sort of container. Redwood baskets or boxes are suitable. So are azalea-type clay pots. I favor these for our climate as the plants seem to do better in them. A 12-inch container takes 2 or 3 plants, plenty for a spectacular show, but I really prefer a 10-inch container with a single plant.

Hanging begonias look best suspended from the branches of a huge old garden tree or from the cross pieces in a high lath house or gazebo. They must have dappled sunlight to make lots of flowers, and wind is the enemy. Frequent feeding is essential for quantities of large blossoms; use a low analysis organic fertilizer. A soluble 6–2–1 formulation is diluted ½ tablespoonful to 1 gallon of water, and you should use this in place of a regular watering at about 2 week intervals. For best results, water your begonias only when traces of dryness appear at the surface of the container. Overwatering leads to root decay and weak plants.

Hanging-basket tuberous begonias vary greatly in blossom form. The European ones tend to be semidouble with large outer petals, rather like their wild ancestor. American ones may resemble these, or they may be fully double. Both are handsome—the double ones make a more voluminous show, but the less full ones bear more flowers. Recently introduced, named, pendulous sorts from a specialist such as Antonelli Brothers make the very best specimens and are well worth the investment once you have developed a good begonia technique.

CASCADE CHRYSANTHEMUMS

The greatest show of hanging plants comes with a fully blown cascade chrysanthemum. I have seen a single plant, grown in one season by a Japanese expert, spread more than 3 feet, with a fall of more than 6 feet! And the entire face of the plant was covered with flowers; scarcely a leaf could be seen. It takes great skill and dedication to achieve such a plant, but any enthusiastic gardener can do a modest cascade or two in his garden.

You must start with chrysanthemum plants of a highly specialized strain. Mine come from Lamb's Nursery (address in the Where to Buy section of this book). Chrysanthemum specialty companies in California also supply these unusual strains.

Through the mail you will get wispy little rooted cuttings looking like nothing at all. Pot them up in a compost of 2 parts fibrous loam and 1 part each leafmold, decayed barnyard manure (or homemade compost), brown peat, and sand. To a bushel of this mixture, add a cupful of superphosphate. Protect the tip of your young plant; you want it to grow straight up. I start mine in 4-inch pots and move them to larger sizes—6-, 8-, 10-inch pots—at 4- to 5-week intervals. The final container size will depend on the bulk of your plant. If you are very successful, you may need a 15-inch tub. Always use clay pots or wood tubs for these.

Real excitement at the garden entrance; a nicely grown cascade-type Japanese chrysanthemum becomes an important feature in the fall garden. From a large terracotta pot the plant grows downward; to show it off, a 6-foot length of cast concrete pipe serves as a pedestal. This fine specimen was grown by Mrs. J. Pancoast Reath for her Philadelphia garden.

When your plant is about 12 inches high, stake it with a 36-inch piece of 12-gauge wire, inserting the stake very close to the trunk of the plant. With strips of rag or wire twists, secure the plant to the stake every 4 inches, from the ground up. Bend the wire and plant to a 45-degree angle at about 6 inches from the soil. Gingerly does it. As side shoots develop, pinch at the third joint, but keep that tip going out along the wire. The plant is grown at this 45°-angle tilt throughout the summer. Some growers favor bending the wire first and training the plant to it; try it both ways.

These cascade chrysanthemums are very late-blooming, so if you live where substantial frosts come in October, begin forcing your plants by covering them with blackout cloth (from a local greenhouse supply company) at 4:00 P.M. in mid-August. At this time, stop all pinching. If you live where the season is long, continue pinching until the end of September. When buds show color on your cascade chrysanthemum, call in a neighbor to help. He will hold the container on a table edge, and you will gently bend down the wire, with plant attached. The bend is made at the original angle, and when you have finished, the tip of the plant should be nearly straight down. Now the plant will come into flower—a cascade of small, daisy-like chrysanthemums, beautiful beyond belief.

Seasonal care makes all the difference with these. Watch the container and add water as soon as any sign of drying appears. On hot, windy days, sagging leaves will tell you that the plant is losing water faster than the roots are taking it up, but if the soil is damp, do not add more water, as decay will set in. The plant will perk up at sundown. Probably a larger container is indicated in a case like this. Continuously moist but never soggy soil is the right condition. Fertilize every 2 weeks, as for tuberous begonias—same solution, same dilution—or spray your plants with a foliar fertilizer such as Ra-Pid-Gro, following the instructions on the container.

If you are very successful, you will have to modify your staking system, as side branches will become heavy and will sag. Add auxiliary stakes, at the same angle as the main stake, to both sides of the container, and add cross pieces at 6 intervals to make a regular trellis. At Bellingrath Gardens in Mobile, Alabama, and at Longwood in Kennett Square, Pennsylvania, the gardeners grow these chrysanthemums on special frames so the plants remain absolutely flat, with every flower showing. I usually end up with plants in 14-inch pots, and I bend a 6-foot piece of 12-gauge wire into a huge hairpin, inserting the ends into the soil against the sides of the pot. A few cross pieces of wire (fastened on with wire twists) carried over the original stake make a suitable support for my modest cascades.

Cascade cultivars are not overly hardy; overwinter your old plants, cut back after frost, pots plunged rim-deep in the coldframe. In early spring fertilize and water them to get strong basal shoots; root these as you do standard garden chrysanthemums when they are a few inches high, and you are on your way for another year of cascade chrysanthemums.

As the seasons change at Longwood Gardens, overhead plants remain an important part of the conservatory display. The photograph right illustrates the summer display with a great column of hanging ivy geraniums; baskets of fuchsias, as well as trailing vines, enhance the hanging garden. Chrysanthemums in baskets and grown as cascades become a spectacular autumn feature, as shown below.

8

How to Plant Boxes, Urns, and Baskets

Having chosen a suitable container, you now must fill it with a growing medium that will give the maximum benefit to your plant or plants. Soil provides nutrients to the roots that grow through it, and, being relatively dense and heavy, provides some anchorage for the plant. But there is more to it: plant roots must grow, therefore the soil must not be too dense. Plant roots must have oxygen, therefore the soil must be porous enough for atmospheric gases to diffuse through it. Roots have to accumulate water for the entire plant, therefore the soil must provide moisture without becoming soggy—water-logged soil contains no air, and roots smother in it. All of this adds up to our having to think in terms of fertility, texture, and density. Perhaps we should learn to call good potting soil "potting compost."

COMPOSTS FOR BOXES, BASKETS, AND URNS

The literature gives dozens of recipes for mixing growing media for containers. While highly refined composts do give extra good results with special plants, I find that a general mixture is handy, and the results satisfactory. I only recommend special composts for choice specimens of tuberous begonias, fuchsias, lantanas, and the like.

My basic mixture is equal parts of soil from the vegetable garden, German peat rubbed through a ¼-inch sieve and shaken over a window-screen sieve to remove dust, and clean river sand (from a builder's-supply company), also shaken over a fine sieve to remove particles. Container-soil mixtures have to be porous, as heavy daily watering is usually necessary, and a soggy condition will develop unless the water runs right through. If your soil has a high clay content, also shake it over a fine screen, to remove the dust. Otherwise it will choke up the drain channels. After the peat is screened twice, spread it and spray it with water. Work it until it is thoroughly dampened before using.

This mixture, just as it stands, suits most plants. Because hot, dry winds blow persistently in the summer in my garden, I add about one fourth, by volume, of coarse perlite to my container compost. This inert material holds a predetermined amount of water, much of which is available to plants if roots attach to the particles. And it does not break down through the season as do some other soil-conditioning materials. Being old-fashioned, I also tamper with the "1 part garden soil." In my composts, this usually is ½ part soil, sifted to remove the clay dust, and ½ well-decayed cow manure, also screened twice. When I omit the composted manure, I notice my plants are more heat-sensitive through midsummer.

To adapt the basic compost for fuchsias, add 1 part composted cow manure (or use commercial leafmold, *not* dehydrated cattle manure), and be sure to include at least a small amount of perlite. This same compost suits tuberous begonias, particularly if a generous amount of fresh hardwood charcoal chips (obtainable at garden shops or drugstores) is mixed through. Gesneriads like this, too.

For lantanas, simply double the amount of sand, and leave in the very fine silt. Lantanas go to leaf if they have a heavy or rich compost. They want a lean, quickly-draining medium, and then you have to water frequently.

PLANTING A BASKET

To me, hanging basket means a carefully made wire basket painted dark green. My objection to plastic "baskets" is that they are too obvious. The point of a basket is the plant in it—not the basket. But you treat them all much the same when it comes to planting.

To keep the compost from spilling out, you must line the basket. Traditionally, fresh sphagnum moss is used, and when carefully handled, it grows on, for at least a time, giving a lively, healthy covering to the underside of the hanging basket. But many of us cannot obtain fresh sphagnum moss, and must make do with something from a package. Fluffy, fairly fresh-looking sphagnum moss *is* available today, packaged in plastic bags. This is a good substitute. I have tried, with reasonable success, peeling sheets of moss from the woods. If you choose a "deep pile" moss and lift it in good-sized patches, and if you supply an inner lining of properly prepared dried sphagnum moss, you come up with quite a nice basket.

With living sphagnum you simply apply handfuls of it—or a sheet of it, if available—to the inner face of the basket. This must be a fairly thick, uninterrupted layer to hold in the potting compost. Dried moss must be soaked for an hour or so, then squeezed out and shaken to fluff it. Apply it as fresh moss. If you buy dried sheet moss, lay it on the terrace and sprinkle it; then cover it with a newspaper for an hour or so. Finally, let it air-dry just enough to handle without pulling it apart.

After you have lined the inside of the basket with a continuous layer of moss, pad the basket with more moistened and squeezed moss until the layer is an inch or more thick. In the dry, windy Middle West, we make our moss layer 2 inches thick at least. When your basket is mossed, you are ready to plant it.

To hold the basket firmly upright while you work, use a large flower pot, partially filled with sand, as a "socket." Lacking a big pot, use a kitchen kettle or a bucket. Pour potting compost into the basket and, with your fingertips, tamp it lightly into the moss. Be careful not to poke a finger through the moss or you will have to stop and make a patch. With the compost worked into the moss, add more compost until the basket is about two thirds full.

Let's presume that this basket is to hold a single specimen plant—fuchsia, begonia, or lantana. Probably this plant will be in a 4- or 5-inch pot.

With the basket partially filled, knock your plant from its container and with a sharp stick tease out enough of the original soil to expose quite a number of root ends. The smaller you can make this earth ball, within reason, the better. Scrape a hole in the center of your basket to take the spread roots. Hold the plant with one hand so its original planting depth is roughly an inch below the rim of the basket, and work compost around the root ball, firming it with your fingertips poked straight downward. Bring the level of the compost up to within an inch of the top of the basket, and the job is done.

The best way to water a newly planted basket is to set it in a tub and bring water about halfway up the sides. As the water soaks through the moss and into the soil, it diffuses upwards. When moisture glistens on the upper surface, the basket is soaked through. Carefully lift it from the water bath and set it aside to drain. A newly planted basket ought to rest in full shade, out of the wind, for at least 3 days before it is hung. As the compost is soaked, additional watering is not necessary until the third or fourth day. But frequent syringing with a fine mist keeps the transplants from wilting too severely. Water a newly set basket moderately for the first 10 days to give the plants time to become established. Apply no fertilizer for 2 weeks, except possibly a very weak solution when you transplant.

Usually, when several plants are placed in a basket, small sizes are used. It is a terrible temptation to cram in enough plants so the finished basket looks fully developed. Don't do it. Crowded plants won't thrive.

Let's plan a mixed "garden" in a 12-inch basket. The basket is mossed, potting compost is worked into the moss, and the basket is almost filled, very loosely, with compost. Take three trailing lobelias from their small pots and space them just at the edge. In the center, plant a bushy browallia, knocked from a 4-inch pot. Between the browallia and the lobelias, and alternating with them, plant three dwarf-type dusty millers. Runners from the lobelias can be spread to either side of the clumps and layered with hairpins to get a broader spread as the plants grow. You will have to pinch back the dusty miller from time to time to keep it from masking the browallia. But you will have a beautiful basket.

Some ferns and ivies look pretty good grown in baskets made of redwood sticks. Moss these baskets just as if they were wire, and plant them the same way. When the ferns push rhizomes out through the sides, your wooden basket will be a real ornament.

MAKING A GLOBE

For those who want a gimmick for the next flower show, let me help you to a fancy display. You will have a globe, completely covered with plants on the outside. Here is how you do it.

Select two matching baskets; they should be the half-round shape that, put together, forms a ball. Moss both of these as for normal planting.

In *one* of the baskets place a small inverted flowerpot and pour potting compost around it to hold it in place. This empty pot, with its opening against the rounded outside of the basket, is important. Fill the basket with potting compost and firm it gently. Lay a board over the basket, grasp the board and the upper wire of the basket with your fingers, and invert. Now you have a mossed, soil-filled half basket inverted on a board. Toenail in a few small brads to secure the basket to the board. This is temporary, so don't drive in the nails too far. Treat the other basket the same way, but omit the flowerpot.

Now trot out that flat of ready-to-bloom young plants. My best results with this foolishness (done in the greenhouse) was with young African-violet plants. But it works with fibrous-rooted begonias, dwarf nasturtiums, bush-form lobelia, and other small compact plants. Use your dibble to poke holes—keep them as small as possible—in the moss and set in the small plants. Space them out to cover both baskets completely, except for the top of the one basket with the flower pot buried just under the moss. Set these baskets in a sheltered spot where plants will grow. When the plants have covered the baskets and are coming into bloom, call in a friend to help you.

First, with your fingers, locate the buried pot and pull away sufficient moss so you can reach the pot with a watering can. This basket will become the top one. Have your friend hold the other basket, now inverted so the plants are down and the board side is up. Set the first basket on top of the second basket so that the two line up. Then remove the brads and slide out the boards *very* gently.

With small pieces of strong wire, fasten the two baskets together. You now have a globe, completely covered with plants! Water it as often as necessary by filling the flowerpot hidden at the top. Suspend it from a single wire—and everybody wonders how on earth you did it.

URNS AND POTS

As you know by this time, I love urns, but I hate to see a beautiful urn stuck into a casual garden. The informal garden calls for pots. Unglazed terra-cotta pots are hard to beat. The handsomest ones come from small towns in Italy and are available from various importers; I favor those warm, dusty-pink ones of terra-rossa pottery. And at least one American company is making a gently flared pot with a rolled rim that rings like a bell when tapped. This one also looks good on the terrace.

Urns or pots, you handle them the same way. Place arched broken crocks over the hole in the bottom (if there is one), add a substantial layer of coarse gravel, crocks, or other inert matter for additional drainage, and fill with soil. The planting technique used for window boxes is applicable to urns and pots.

Build up a collection of similar pots in various sizes. Avoid anything smaller than 10 inches in diameter. Then, build up a collection of plants to fill the pots. A pendent fuchsia, grown as a standard, goes in the largest one. A weeping lantana, decumbent rosemary, a pot of twining, dangling nasturtiums, a pot on the wall, with burro's-tail sedum braiding its way downward—these can make up the bulk of your collection. Better include a few pots of upright plants or people will think you were born under a weeping willow. In winter, most of these plants go into the bright entryway. There they decorate pedestals, plant stands, or brackets.

WATERING CONTAINER-GROWN PLANTS

Soil around the roots of a plant must never get completely dry; most flowering plants do best when the soil is damp but not water-logged. So it is with pendent plants grown in hanging baskets, window boxes, urns, and terrace pots. They have to be watered enough for them to make shoots and new buds throughout the growing season.

Hanging baskets dry out very quickly. The plants take up water for photosynthesis and also lose a considerable amount through evaporation from the leaves. Furthermore, the mossy layer lining the container acts as a wick, drawing water from the potting compost to be lost by evaporation at the surface of the basket. On windy days, even though the basket hangs in a fairly sheltered spot, water loss may be extreme. I have had to water fuchsias and lantanas as often as 3 times daily in my garden; this is asking for trouble because the soil may get soggy. After having suffered several sad losses of plants, I now take down my baskets when the wind blows unremittingly and set them in the sheltered shrubbery until the gale is past.

Window boxes and porch boxes also require frequent watering on hot or breezy days. In these containers only a small amount of potting compost supports a quantity of leafy plants. While the amount of water lost through the sides of the container probably is negligible, the foliar water loss may be great. Boxes in mist-bathed Seattle may need water only 2 or 3 times a week, but in my Middle West garden they get a generous flooding each morning, shortly after sunup, and they are checked at noon if the day seems particularly hot or windy.

A number of factors affects the rate of water loss from baskets, boxes, and urns: the ratio of soil volume to leafy plants; the water-retentive qualities of the soil; the *kind* of plant—lantanas require tremendous amounts of water while tuberous begonias, though demanding constant dampness, take up much less. When you grow plants in containers, there is just one rule to follow: inspect them frequently, watering pot in hand; if the soil approaches dryness, give water.

Plants in large pots and urns usually take less water than those in baskets and boxes because the volume of soil is greater. Even so, never let them go too long without checking. Once plants have wilted, bloom will be sparse for some weeks to come.

It is a temptation to use heavy soil, generously fortified with moisture-holding peat, in order to solve this water problem with container-grown plants. But many plants resent heavy soils; too much peat not only gives an excessively "organic" soil for some plants, but may lead to a soggy condition. The one substance that helps most in my garden is perlite. This synthetic, non-deteriorating, spongy product holds a remarkable amount of water without detracting from the porosity of the soil. Perlite, as much as a third by volume, can be added to a potting compost to enhance its water-retaining characteristics before the growth of most plants is adversely affected. Where days are hot and dry winds blow, the use of perlite in the soil mixture can mean the difference between success and failure.

USE OF FERTILIZER

Fertilizing plants in window boxes, porch boxes, hanging baskets, garden urns, and terrace pots depends somewhat on the soil employed to make the basic compost. Most annuals used for boxes, urns, and pots do best in only moderately fertile soil; too much fertilizer, particularly too much nitrogen, results in lots of soft green leaves and only a few flowers.

But even the best of soils will be worn out before summer is past. Some feeding is essential if plants are to look their best right up to frost. I recommend planting in a fairly lean mixture—already given—with little or no fertilizer used at planting time. A drink made up of high-phosphate transplant solution will encourage early root expansion; then let the roots go looking for nutrients. When new shoots begin to appear on plants, start a regular feeding regimen.

For begonias, fuchsias, and a few other special plants, I alternate between a dilute solution of fish emulsion and liquid manure. The plants are fertilized each week—large ones twice a week—a few hours after they are watered. The fish emulsion comes in a bottle or gallon can and I make up the recommended solution, then reduce it with additional water to two-thirds or half strength. I hang a cloth bag of dehydrated cattle manure in a large crock of rain water and dilute the resulting fluid to a pale tea-colored liquid. Both of these fertilizers produce prize-winning baskets; I alternate them on the theory that one will supply what the other may lack.

My window boxes and terrace pots do very nicely with commercial house-plant fertilizer—the kind you measure out as a crystalline powder and dissolve in water. Again, I dilute the chemical rather more than recommended on the package, and I switch from one brand to another to take advantage of the best qualities of several kinds. Never apply a liquid fertilizer solution to dry potting soil; this can result in severe root damage. Water your plants regularly, then, a few hours later, give them their liquid fertilizer solution. I usually discontinue feeding plants I wish to save over winter about a month to 6 weeks before first frost date. This hardens them somewhat so they move indoors more easily.

INSECTS AND DISEASES

I have experienced few pests and diseases with my basket and box plants, with some notable exceptions. Among the insects, aphids and white fly are a first-class trial, and crown-rot disease is a serious problem for me because hot days raise the soil temperature so that parasitic fungi thrive.

Usually I try to control aphids and white fly with a sharp spray from the hose, especially in late evening. Insecticides would be easier and more efficient, but we keep bees and the hummingbirds feed at many of our flowers. If a basket or box seems to be overly infested, I spray with a garden insecticide preparation of Meta-Systox-R, a systemic, that gets rid of all sucking insects for about 6 weeks. After spraying, I cover the plants with a single layer of cheesecloth for one day to keep bees and birds away. Then all is safe again. But you must be sure to use a preparation with just the systemic. Many common garden insecticides are shotgun mixtures and the non-systemic chemicals are extremely toxic to beneficial insects and hummingbirds.

Toward fall—our hummingbirds head for South America in late August—I spray more frequently, attempting to get rid of all white fly and spider mites so that geranium, lantana, and cape-plumbago cuttings will go inside clean, and so that fuchsia, lantana, and begonia plants will not carry their little parasites indoors.

Occasionally a cutworm moth lays eggs in a window box and we lose a few petunias, lobelias, and verbenas. Or a leaf-gnawing "worm" of some sort defoliates a shoot. When this happens, the search is on. I am a firm believer in direct retribution and capital punishment. It takes only a few minutes to find the culprit and squash it on a rock—much more satisfactory than chemical warfare.

Rarely a little mildew shows up on a few tuberous-begonia leaves; I have also had both mildew and a tiny leafspot disease on fuchsia. In both cases, a "complete" spray for roses, applied on my way to the rose garden, brought the problem under control quickly. After all, one of the best ways to avoid mildews and leafspot diseases is good air circulation, and with hanging plants air circulation should be optimum.

But crown rot is something else. One day a petunia is crisp, thriving, and full of flowers; a day later the foliage is gray-green and drooping. The next day the plant is dead. Examination shows the stems to be blanched and scraped-looking at the ground line. This can happen to almost any other soft-stemmed plant. And where the soil heats up, it does happen.

Crown rot is caused by an insidious group of fungi that are extremely difficult to kill. *Rhizoctonia, Pythium,* and *Phytopthora* fungi all may be involved. No single fungicide presently marketed for home use will adequately control all three of these. But I have found that Dexon solution gives quite good protection. I also have used Pano-Drench with good results. Terrachlor is satisfactory in early spring when the weather is cool and the soil chilly (it is good all summer in cool climates), but when the soil warms up, some plants are put in stress by the heat. My technique is to water in newly set plants with a suitable solution of one of the above fungicides; this usually keeps a box or other container clean through summer.

9

Notes on Propagation

Every gardener worth his salt likes to grow his own plants. This is not to say that all of us do not dream of being situated so we could finance and care for vast lists of new plants ordered from specialists' catalogues and picked up at the local nursery. Some hanging plants can be propagated at home; others should be purchased.

The sort of plant used for the indoor hanging garden does not, in my estimation, lend itself to propagation from seed. That statement will get me considerable correspondence quite regularly from clever little old ladies who produce quantities of columneas, episcias, vining ficuses, and other rarities from seed under lights in their basements. But for the average homeowner I recommend visiting the local specialist; study the shapes, colors, and textures of leaves of his hanging plants (always consider flowers a bonus—they come and go, but the leaves are there always) and make a selection. No doubt you will bring home twice as many as you have room for, and will live on hamburger for a month. It's worth it.

As always, there are exceptions. If you have a plant room or a cool, bright bay window, probably you will want baskets of canary-bird-vine, nasturtiums, passion-vines, and the like. These are easy to grow from seed, and it would be foolish to buy plants. On the other hand, if you want an exceptionally nice ivy geranium or have your heart set on a 'Swingtime' fuchsia, you must remember that these named cultivars do not come true from seed; they have to be grown from cuttings, so you must obtain a cutting and root it, or buy a plant already started.

One way to save money is to buy dormant material whenever possible. A first-class dormant tuberous begonia corm runs twenty-five to fifty cents. The same thing, potted up and growing as a leafy plant at the greenhouse, will be a dollar or more. This holds true for achimenes, caladiums, oxalis, and other tuberous, cormaceous, or bulbous species used as hanging plants. When you buy dormant material, don't run home and stick it in the middle of a basket or box. Tuberous begonia corms should first be sprouted in a flat of barely damp peat, then potted up to become established before going into the basket, as discussed in Chapter 7. Caladiums are handled similarly. Oxalis and achimines should be started in small pots and, when growing well, transplanted to the container in which they are to bloom.

GROWING FROM SEED

Geraniums, coleus, hybrid lantanas, verbenas, and a host of other first-class plants for outdoor baskets, boxes, and urns are easy from seed. One way is to go the modern route: Set up a bank of fluorescent lights in the basement, buy a bag of Jiffy-Sevens, and the trays they are set in, and carry on from there. The other, more traditional, way is to make up a germinating compost of some sort—natural or synthetic—fill flats or bulb pans with it, sow your seeds, and grow the seedlings under lights, on the window sill, or in the backyard greenhouse. Both ways have advantages and disadvantages; by trial and error, you will find which works best for your situation.

Put the young plants in individual pots; most make better specimens if pinched once or twice while quite young to insure their becoming bushy. When they look as if they are ready to bud, move them to the box, terrace pot, garden urn, or hanging basket in which they are to bloom.

Geranium, tuberous begonia, asparagus-fern and sprengeri

asparagus, and fibrous-rooted begonia seed should be started soon after New Year's, as these are slow and take months to reach the point of making a show. Other annuals, or plants grown as annuals, should be started from seed 6 to 8 weeks prior to planting-out time. If you start seeds too early you may end up with weak, spindly plants unless your growing conditions are quite good.

I use Jiffy-Sevens (starting pots of compressed organic material) for Carefree geranium seed and one or two other things. Soak the de-hydrated containers in water for several hours until they swell; set them in a small watertight tray. With a pencil, make two small holes in each, poke in two seeds (insurance) and work the holes shut. Place the containers in a 70° F. place, and keep them moist.

Most seed at my home is started in John Innes germinating compost; the formula is given in garden encyclopedias and reference works. It is based on pasteurized loam, and, in my opinion, gives the sturdiest, most normal seedlings of any germinating medium. But you may resort to the easier-to-prepare synthetic mixtures, many of which are available already blended. Whatever your medium, place it in a presoaked, clean, terra-cotta bulb pan (squatty flower pot), and let it draw water from below until the surface is damp. Sow your seed; fine seed is left uncovered, but cover coarser seed to about twice its diameter with more of the growing medium. Stretch a piece of clear plastic over the pot and hold it down with a rubber band. Set in a 70° F. place for germination, and as quickly as seedlings appear, move to bright light. Pokes holes in the plastic a few days after germination, and a day or two later remove it entirely.

CUTTINGS

Cuttings are the easiest and least expensive way of building up a collection of fine plants. Soft-stemmed plants, such as coleus, im-patiens, and most gesneriads, root readily in a glass of water. When rooting plants in water, you may experience difficulty in transferring them to soil. Pot up when roots are only ½-inch long. And do not overwater.

Verbenas, petunias, geraniums, lantanas, sultanas, cape plumbago, fuchsias, all gesneriads, true ivies, Swedish-ivy, and a host of other trailing plants root readily in a most, porous, solid medium. Sand was commonly used in the old days. Today I prefer straight No. 2 horticultural-grade perlite or a mixture of perlite and German brown peat rubbed through a 1/4-inch screen and shaken over a fine sieve to remove the dust. Peat should always be moistened before incorporating with perlite, soil, or other ingredients.

Prepare a 4-inch-deep container—with good bottom drainage—for your cuttings by filling with rooting medium. Take cuttings with a sharp knife or, better, a single-edged razor blade; clip off leaves to expose about 2 inches of stem and dip the fresh cut end in rooting hormone. With a pencil, poke a hole in the rooting medium and stick in the cutting. Space cuttings so leaves just touch but do not crowd. When the container is filled, gently flood the medium with clean, cool (about 70° F.) water and set it in a bright north window at room temperature. To reduce water loss from the leaves, drape a thin piece of clear plastic over the cuttings and pot. In 2 to 3 days, move the pot to a sunny place. If the cuttings wilt excessively, place them farther back from the window. In a few days, remove the plastic at night and, finally, leave it off altogether. Do not overwater the cuttings, but keep the medium damp.

When roots on the cuttings reach a length of 1/2 inch to 3/4 inch, pot up. I like to pinch newly potted cuttings as this reduces the leafy surface (which loses water), and cuttings take hold faster. Also, branching begins immediately.

DIVISIONS

A few pendent plants form the sort of clump that can be divided when you have an urge for more plants. Swedish-ivy, Kenilworth-ivy, *Vinca major variegata,* and airplane-plant are examples of plants that develop a cluster of crowns on a rather creeping, more-or-less-underground rhizome. This cluster can be pulled or cut apart, breaking a large clump up into 3 or 4 pieces, each with stems and roots. These parts are potted up independently. Old clumps of the ornamental asparaguses divide readily; as the rhizomes of these are very tough, use a stout clippers or lopping shears to cut the clump apart.

A few choice basket plants multiply by increasing tubers or bulbs. Some oxalis species are bulbous, and as a clump goes out of bloom, you can dry it off, lift the bulbs, and reset them separately. Achimenes grow from woolly, wormlike scaly tubers. Dry off the plants somewhat in the fall, finally cut them back, and let them cure in the soil. In spring, knock them free of soil and pot them up separately to make lots of new plants for summer boxes and baskets. Be gentle. These tubers are brittle as glass. And plant every little piece, as most will grow.

Glossary of Terms

ANNUAL A plant that grows from seed to maturity, sets seed, and dies in a single season. Zinnias are true annuals; snapdragons and fibrous-rooted begonias are frost-sensitive perennials used as annuals.

BASKET A (usually) bowl-shaped container for plants that is suspended by wires or light chain. Once almost exclusively made of wire, these now may be of plastic, wood, or other material. For best appearance, choose baskets that are unobtrusive and will not detract from the plants.

BULB PAN Flower pots less than half the height of the standard pot; usually less than half as high as the face diameter of the pot. These are excellent for use in germinating seed.

CHARCOAL Hardwood charcoal, usually available at garden shops and at the drugstore, is an excellent absorbing agent. It is used in potting composts for plants with sensitive roots or where water is heavily mineralized. Do not use crumbled hardwood charcoal briquets as these are made with toxic binding chemicals.

COMPOST (1) Decomposed vegetable debris; make it in the garden by building up repeated layers of discarded plant materials, soil mixed with a little animal manure, and a trace of chemical fertilizer. (2) A special potting or growing medium that contains organic matter, as a "potting compost" where specific ingredients are used in predetermined amounts.

CROCK Broken pieces of terra-cotta flower pots, usually placed for better drainage in the bottom of containers. Cover the pot hole with a curved piece of crock so water runs out freely but soil is obstructed; then add a layer of smaller pieces of crock for further drainage.

CULTIVAR   A term used to describe a plant that has been created in cultivation and that is maintained only in cultivation—opposed to VARIETY which is a plant that occurs naturally and may be found growing naturally.

CUTTING   A plant part, stem, root, or leaf, removed for the purpose of growing another plant like the parent. Sometimes referred to as a SLIP.

DECUMBENT   Tending to grow downward; as the "weeping" branches of a birch tree or a basket fuchsia.

DIBBLE   Hand tool, L-shaped or curved, with the short leg as the handle, and the longer piece coming to a sharp point, for making planting holes.

EPIPHYTE   Plants that grow with their roots not in soil. Usually perched on trees, these depend on high humidity and their own highly specialized roots for sustenance. Spanish-moss and orchids, in trees, are examples. In culture these are usually grown on a slab of wood or osmunda, or are "planted" in an inert, well-aerated medium, such as fir bark, osmunda, or chopped moss.

FORCE   (1) To induce a plant to develop and flower out of season. (2) To encourage rapid growth with optimum cultural techniques such as frequent fertilizing, careful watering, and so on.

HYBRID   The result of cross-breeding individuals from different species. Most garden and greenhouse plants are hybrids of complex parentage.

LEAFMOLD   Partially decomposed leaves; useful for various potting composts after the leafmold has been rubbed through ¼-inch sieve. Where disease or pests may be a problem, pasteurize before using by steaming (no pressure) in a covered roaster in the oven until an oven thermometer registers 180° F. for 10 minutes.

LOAM   Technically, a soil composed of more-or-less equal parts silt and sand and less than 20 percent clay. It should be firm, but mellow, with sufficient humus to stimulate vigorous plant growth.

PEAT   Partially decomposed, and chemically altered, plant parts derived chiefly from bog sedges and mosses. While peat may contain moss parts (as does coal) the term "peat moss" is absolutely erroneous. Irish and German peats are best for horticultural use, Canadian peat is good though usually overmilled to dust, and Michigan peat has some value as a source of humus.

PERENNIAL   A plant that lives several years; technically this includes trees and shrubs, but to the gardener, a perennial plant is nonwoody.

PINCH   To remove the growing tip of a stem, thus inducing branching. Usually done with small clippers or fingertips.

POT   A container for plants. Terra-cotta (fired clay) pots, long in use, permit some air movement from the outside to the soil they contain, and, being porous, they allow water to escape, cooling the container. Plastic pots now are favored by some growers; these require potting composts that are quite porous.

POT-BOUND   Describes the condition when roots of a plant have filled the potting soil and then grown round and round just inside the pot until completely entangled so growth slows or stops. In repotting, a pot-bound plant's roots must be untangled and clipped back; prune the top to maintain a proper proportion of leafy top to root.

RUNNER   A stolon. A horizontal stem that roots at the tip or at the joints, and produces plants at these points. Some episcias, the strawberry-begonia, and some potentillas make runners.

SAND   Particles of rock, larger than silt and smaller than pebbles; useful to speed up aeration and drainage of potting composts. The best sands are of particles with sharp edges. Clean river sand such as used for mortar and concrete are suitable for horticultural purposes. Crushed granite (sold as Baby Chick Granite Grit) is extremely valuable for special cases.

SPECIES   The term used to designate a group of closely related plants. A plant family, the gesneriad family, for example (*Gesneriaceae*) contains a number of Genera (singular, Genus), as the African-violet or *Saintpaulia*, the flame-violet or *Episcia*, and the nut orchid, *Achimenes*. Each of these is divided into groups of closely related plants, the species, as *Saintpaulia ionantha*. Garden-derived offspring of a species are cultivars, as African-violet 'Blue Boy'.

SPHAGNUM MOSS   A genus of mosses, usually growing in bogs, that are horticulturally useful either fresh or dried, as they grow into fairly tight mats that are convenient for lining baskets to hold the soil. Or the moss can be rubbed to powder and incorporated in germinating composts.

STOLON   See RUNNER.

Where to Buy

This is *my* list of sources; probably many companies not included offer similar or even superior products. But I list only those with whom I have dealt or whose materials and plants I have encountered somewhere along the line. Source lists, to be appended at the end of a book, are a great trial; companies come and go; addresses change. But I feel that I must offer a source list to save on correspondence. Let me suggest that when you write to these companies, you slip a dollar bill in the envelope to cover the cost of a catalog or price list and postage. Probably you will get it back with your first purchase.

Alpenglow Gardens
13328 King George Highway
North Surrey, British Columbia,
Canada

fuchsias and hardy plants

Antonelli Bros. Begonia Gardens
2545 Capitola Road
Santa Cruz, California 95062

tuberous begonias, fuchsias, achimenes

Beahm Gardens
2686 East Paloma Street
Pasadena, California 91107

epiphyllums, other cacti, hoyas

Ernst Benary Blaupunkt Samen
351 Hann. Muenden
Postfach 109
West Germany

fibrous-rooted begonia seed and
other seed (will correspond in English)

W. Atlee Burpee Co.
Box 6929
Philadelphia, Pennsylvania 19132

seeds, some bulbs, corms, and tubers

Cook's Geranium Nursery
712 North Grand
Lyons, Kansas 67554

geraniums, including scented, ivy,
zonal, and others

P. de Jager & Sons, Inc.
188 Asbury Street
South Hamilton, Massachusetts
01982

hardy and tender bulbs, corms, and
tubers

Edelweiss Gardens
Box 66
Robbinsville, New Jersey 08691

house plants, ferns, cacti, orchids,
supplies

George Schenk Wild Gardens
8243 N.E. 119th Street
Kirkland, Washington 98033

native trailing and creeping plants

Lamb Nurseries
East 101 Sharp Avenue
Spokane, Washington 99202

cascade chrysanthemums, herbs,
other hardy plants

Logee's Greenhouses
55 North Street
Danielson, Connecticut 06239

house plants in great variety

Manhattan Garden Supply
305 N. Sepulveda Blvd.
Manhattan Beach, California 90266

fuchsias, geraniums, tuberous begonias, supplies

Merry Gardens
Camden, Maine 04843

house plants in great variety

Neilson Bromeliads   bromeliads in variety
225 San Bernardino
North Fort Myers, Florida 33903

Oakhurst Gardens   rare hardy and tender plants, bulbs,
P.O. Box 444   corms and tubers
Arcadia, California 91006

George W. Park Seed Company, Inc.   seeds, bulbs, corms, tubers, house
Greenwood, South Carolina 29646   plants, supplies

Roehrs Exotic Nurseries   house plants in great variety
East Rutherford,
New Jersey 07073

Sunnybrook Farm Nursery   herbs, some gesneriads, sedums, and
9448 Mayfield Road   hardy plants
Chesterland, Ohio 44026

Van Bourgondien Brothers   hardy and tender bulbs, corms, and
P.O. Box A   tubers
Babylon, New York 11702

Vetterle & Reinelt   tuberous begonias
P.O. Box 125
Capitola, California 95010

Walter Nicke   English hanging baskets, supplies
Hudson, New York 12534

The Wayside Gardens Company   bulbs, corms, tubers, fuchsias, tuber-
Mentor, Ohio 44060   ous begonias, and many other
                                      plants; baskets and other supplies

White Flower Farm   bulbs, corms, tubers, fuchsias, tuber-
Litchfield, Connecticut 06759   ous begonias, some other hardy
                                      plants, Terra-Rossa pottery, baskets

Index

[*Figures in italics denote illustrations*]

Photo Credits

John Philip Baumgardt: pages 12, 13, 14, 15, 16
Burpee Seed Company: page 73 bottom
William J. Cook: pages 77, 83, 97
Flower and Garden Magazine: pages 10, 28 top, 29, 53, 56, 76
Fred Galle, Calloway Gardens: pages 28 bottom, 47, 48, 57, 75
Gilchrist for Ernesta Drinker Ballard: pages 3 right, 18, 21, 22, 23, 99
Longwood Gardens: pages 68 bottom, 101
Merry Gardens: pages 32, 33, 36, 37, 38, 45
Pan-American Seed Company: pages 73 top left and right, 92
George Taloumis: pages 11 left, 68 top, 69 top, 70
Vinceguerra for Ernesta Drinker Ballard: page 63 bottom